Cambridge
Collections

WITHDRAWN

Who we are

a citizenship collection

Edited by Geoff Barton
Series editor : Michael Marland

CAMBRIDGE
U

CAMBRIDGE UNIVERSITY PRESS

Cambridge, New York, Melbourne, Madrid, Cape Town, Singapore, São Paulo, Delhi

Cambridge University Press
The Edinburgh Building, Cambridge CB2 8RU, UK

www.cambridge.org
Information on this title: www.cambridge.org/9780521703154

© Cambridge University Press 2007

First published 2007

Printed in the United Kingdom at the University Press, Cambridge

A catalogue record for this publication is available from the British Library

ISBN 978-0-521-70315-4 paperback

Cover image: Vladimir/Shutterstock

Cover design by Smith

Illustrations by Julia Pearson/Beehive Illustration

Picture research by Sandie Huskinson-Rolfe of PHOTOSEEKERS

Acknowledgements

The authors and publishers acknowledge the following sources of copyright material and are grateful for the permissions granted. While every effort has been made, it has not always been possible to identify the sources of all the material used, or to trace all copyright holders. If any omissions are brought to our notice, we will be happy to include the appropriate acknowledgements on reprinting.

p. 3 *Clara's Day* by Penelope Lively from *Pack of Cards: Collected Short Stories 1978–1986*, copyright © 1986 Penelope Lively, published by Heinemann, reproduced by permission of David Higham Associates on behalf of the author; p. 9 *Sliding* by Leslie Norris, copyright © 1978 Leslie Norris, reproduced by permission of Combrógos Literary Agency; p. 18 *Taming the Tiger* by Tony Anthony & Angela Little, copyright © Authentic Media 2004, reproduced by permission of Authentic Media; p. 24 *I Wish I Were . . .* by Rabindranath Tagore, reproduced by permission of Visva-Bharati; p. 27 *I Was Left with a Childcarer . . . and Never Collected* by Barbara Brown from *The Guardian Weekend*, 10 June 2006, reproduced by permission of Guardian Newspapers Limited; p. 38 *My Best Teacher*, interview with Vic Reeves, by Marged Richards from *The Times Educational Supplement*, 6 June 2006, reproduced by permission of Marged Richards (www.margedrichards.com); p. 41 *The Secret Life of Snap Decisions* by Malcolm Gladwell from *Blink*, copyright © 2005 Malcolm Gladwell, print rights reproduced by permission of Penguin Group (UK) and Little, Brown, electronic rights reproduced by permission of Janklow & Nesbit Associates, on behalf of the author; p. 44 *The Selfish Giant* by Oscar Wilde (1884–1900), this version appears in *Complete Shorter Fiction*, published by Oxford University Press; p. 50 *An African Elegy* by Ben Okri from *An African Elegy*, published by Jonathan Cape, 1992, reproduced by permission of The Marsh Agency Ltd on behalf of the poet; p. 54 *I Found Love at the Supermarket Checkout* by Tom Hill from *The Guardian Weekend*, 24 June 2006, reproduced by permission of Guardian Newspapers Limited; p. 58 *Warning to Children* by Robert Graves from *Collected Poems*, copyright © 1975, reproduced by permission of Carcanet Press Limited; p. 68 *If* by Rudyard Kipling (1865–1936), this version appears in *A Choice of Kipling's Verse* by T S Eliot, published by Faber and Faber; p. 70 *Through the Tunnel* by Doris Lessing from *In the Habit of Loving*, copyright © 1954 Doris Lessing, reprinted by kind permission of Jonathan Clowes Ltd, on behalf of Doris Lessing; p. 81 *Almost Drowning* by Richard Branson from *Losing My Virginity: the Autobiography*, published by Virgin Books, copyright © Richard Branson 1998, 2002, 2005, reproduced by permission of Virgin Books Ltd; p. 85 *The Boy Who Fell Out of the Sky* by Ken Dornstein, copyright © 2006 Ken Dornstein, reproduced by permission of Hodder and Stoughton Limited and Random House Inc.; p. 92 *Once in a House on Fire* by Andrea Ashworth, copyright © 1998 Andrea Ashworth, published by Pan Macmillan, print rights reproduced by permission of Pan Macmillan, electronic and audio rights reproduced by permission of Michelle Kass Associates on behalf of the author; p. 96 *My Mam's Death* by Samantha Studley from *True to Life*, edited by Susan Hemmings, published by Sheba Feminist Press 1986; p. 109 *The Year 1000* by Robert Lacey and Danny Danziger from *What Life Was Like at the Turn of the First Millennium*, copyright © 1999 Robert Lacey and Danny Danziger, published by Little, Brown, reproduced by permission of Little, Brown; p. 113 *Down the Mine* by George Orwell from *Inside the Whale*, copyright © 1933 George Orwell, reproduced by permission of Bill Hamilton as the Literary Executor of the Estate of the Late Sonia Brownell Orwell, and Secker & Warburg Ltd; p. 121 *The Village Blacksmith* by Henry Wadsworth Longfellow (1807–1882), this version is taken from *Collins Book of Best Loved Verse*, published by Collins; p. 124 *MCMXIV* by Philip Larkin from *Collected Poems*, published by Faber and Faber, reproduced by permission of Faber and Faber Ltd; p. 127 *The Roses of No Man's Land* by Lyn MacDonald, copyright © 1980 Lyn MacDonald, published by Michael Joseph 1980, print rights reproduced by permission of Penguin Group (UK), electronic and audio rights reproduced by permission of Pollinger Limited on behalf of Lyn MacDonald; p, 134 *Not My Best Side* by U. A. Fanthorpe from *Collected Poems 1978–2003*, published by Peterloo Poets, 2005, reproduced by permission of Peterloo Poets; p. 147 *The Destructors* by Graham Greene from *Twenty-One Stories*, published by Random House, copyright © 1954 Graham Greene, reproduced by permission of David Higham Associates; p. 164 *We Are Going to See the Rabbit (After Prévert)* by Alan Brownjohn from *Collected Poems*, published by Enitharmon Press, 2006, reproduced by permission of Enitharmon Press; p. 167 *Song of the Battery Hen* by Edwin Brock, published by Secker & Warburg, 1977, reproduced by permission of David Higham Associates; p. 169 *Alexander Graham Bell and the Telephone* by Adam Hart-Davis and Paul Bader from *100 Local Heroes*, published by Sutton Publishing, 1997, copyright © Adam Hart-Davis and Paul Bader, reproduced by kind permission of Adam Hart-Davis and Paul Bader; p. 173 *Hunger* by Laurence Binyon, reproduced by permission of The Society of Authors as the Literary Representative of the Estate of Laurence Binyon; p. 175 *What the All-American Meal is Doing to the World* by Eric Schlosser, copyright © 2001 by Eric Schlosser, originally published in *Fast Food Nation*, reprinted by permission of the author; p. 183 *Facts to Change the World* by Jessica Williams from *50 Facts that Should Change the World*, published by Icon Books, Cambridge, 2004, reproduced by permission of Icon Books Ltd; p. 189 *Somebody's Watching You* by Alexandra Campbell, from *The Daily Telegraph*, 29 May 2004, copyright © The Telegraph, reproduced by permission of The Telegraph Media Group Limited; p. 195 *Televised* by Maya Angelou from *I Shall Not be Moved*, copyright © 1990 Maya Angelou, reproduced by permission of Little, Brown, Random House Inc. and Helen Brann Agency Inc. on behalf of the author; p. 197 *The Fish Are All Sick* by Anne Stevenson from *Poems 1955–2005*, published by Bloodaxe Books, reproduced by permission of Bloodaxe Books; p. 198 *The Lake* by Roger McGough from *Holiday on Death Row*, copyright © 1979 Roger McGough, reproduced by permission of PFD (www.pfd.co.uk) on behalf of Roger McGough; p. 200 *Before Eden* by Arthur C. Clarke from *Tales of Ten Worlds*, published by Gollancz 2003, reproduced by permission of David Higham Associates on behalf of the author.

The publishers would like to thank the following for permission to reproduce photographs: 29, Jean Goldsmith 2006; 50, Sutton-Hibbert/Rex Features; 56, Michelle Sank 2006; 86, © PA Photos; 114, 169, Getty Images; 126, The Art Archive/Imperial War Museum; 136, © National Gallery, London/The Bridgeman Art Library; 167, Vario Images GmbH & Co.KG/Alamy; 185, © Peter Turnley/CORBIS.

Contents

General introduction

Who we are is about just that – who we are. It is a collection of stories, poems and non-fiction texts that explore what it is like to be human. How are we different from animals? How do we feel and think? Where have we come from? Where are we heading?

It's a collection designed to link with some of the issues you may be thinking about in Citizenship and PSHE, such as rights, responsibilities, identity and tradition. But this is very definitely a book to read and enjoy in English lessons, with lots of activities designed to help you explore not only the issues but also the language of the texts. It is divided into five sections:

Growing pains gets you thinking about where you came from. What kind of young child were you? Who influenced you? What are your earliest memories? You'll encounter texts about other people's childhoods, both real and imagined. How did their experiences shape the person they grew up to be?

Letting go is about how we all start to want to become independent – about how we start to take control of our own lives, the advice we are given and the choices we make. There are memories, celebrations of influential people and descriptions of the way we start to grow apart from other people, as well as accounts of the sort of unexpected events that can catch us by surprise.

Facing the world begins with a poem of advice from Rudyard Kipling, and then shows human beings in difficult circumstances – facing challenges that have tested their courage, character and self-belief.

Britain in the past is exactly that – a section that explores who we were and shows us some of the features of our history. We cannot really know who we are if we don't know something about where we come from. You'll travel down a 20th-century coal mine and see other work that was once an essential part of everyday life but has now almost vanished. You'll share the insights of people who lived through World War I and even explore the battle between George and the dragon from the point of view of the dragon.

The world about us looks at the world we are creating. It touches on some of the big issues facing your generation, the changing nature of the media and our responsibilities as global citizens to the other humans on this fragile planet.

Within these five sections, the texts are arranged so that the more difficult ones are placed at the end of the section. To support your reading, certain words (these are numbered) in the text are explained in the footnotes. Ideas for further reading accompany each text. Each section concludes with a range of reading, writing, speaking, listening and drama activities to help you explore and enjoy the authors' ideas, opinions, style and language.

Through this exploration you will, I hope, gain an insight into what makes a good text work, in terms of its structure and content, and think about what we can learn from the situations the characters find themselves in. The text-specific activities pages are divided into the following activity types: *Before you read* (pre-reading stimulation activities), *What's it about?* (comprehension-style questions) and *Thinking about the text* (activities which move beyond the text itself). At the very end of each section, a series of *Compare and contrast* activities provide opportunities to directly compare two or more texts.

I hope very much you'll enjoy the range of texts. There's certainly a huge variety, including stories, poems, autobiographical writing, biography, articles, arguments and descriptions.

Some of the texts were written specifically for people of your age. Most of them weren't. But the book has been put together with you firmly in mind, to interest, entertain and even occasionally inspire you. It should also, I hope, help you to celebrate the joy and pain of who we are – human beings coping with a complicated, often confusing, world of endless, exciting and terrifying change.

Geoff Barton

1 Growing pains

In this section you will find a range of poetry, fiction and non-fiction texts, all of which examine the world of childhood in different ways. When adults talk about childhood, they often present it as a world of bright, innocent sunshine and perpetual happiness. We all know that childhood can be like that at times, but we should also remember that children have their fair share of troubles and worries.

This section helps you to explore the nature of childhood. In particular you will read about:

- the experiences that can shape our future
- the skills and qualities people can develop
- the impact school can have on a child's life.

These texts will also encourage you to think about your own childhood – the good and the bad bits, and how these have influenced you in your life so far.

Activities

1 Take a blank piece of paper or a page in your English exercise book. Spend two minutes thinking about your earliest memories. Draw a doodle or write a word or phrase for each memory that comes back to you as you read these memory kick-starters:

- your earliest memory
- the first Christmas present you remember
- playing outside
- food you liked/disliked
- a place you especially remember
- a teacher who sticks in your mind
- a toy or game you especially remember
- a holiday
- getting in trouble.

2 School is important to us in our early years – it's where we develop our confidence, learn new skills and make friends. Use a spider diagram to collect memories of your nursery or primary school. Think about the teachers, the rooms, the activities, the smell, the colours and anything else you recall about your early experience.

3   The writer L. P. Hartley wrote: 'The past is a foreign country: they do things differently there.' Looking back, does your childhood seem like a different world? Using the notes you made in activities 1 and 2, describe your childhood to a partner. While your partner is talking, write down the key points about his or her early life.

Now discuss what you have remembered. Use these questions to help you:

- What were the best and worst features of her or his childhood?
- What does she or he remember most vividly?
- What does she or he see in your character now that can be traced back to when s/he was very young?

Clara's Day

by Penelope Lively

> This story by Penelope Lively shows how our emotional lives at home can sometimes have an impact on the way we behave in school.

When Clara Tilling was 15½ she took off all her clothes one morning in school assembly. She walked naked through the lines of girls, past the headmistress and the other staff, and out into the entrance lobby. She had left off her bra and pants already, so all she had to do was unbutton her blouse, remove it and drop it to the floor, and then undo the zipper of her skirt and let that fall. She slipped her feet out of her shoes at the same time and so walked barefoot as well as naked. It all happened very quickly. One or two girls giggled and a sort of rustling noise ran through the assembly hall, like a sudden wind among trees. The Head hesitated for a moment – she was reading out the tennis team list – and then went on again, firmly. Clara opened the big glass doors and let herself out.

The entrance lobby was empty. The floor was highly polished and she could see her own reflection, a foreshortened pink blur. There was a big bright modern painting on one wall and several comfortable chairs for waiting parents, arranged round an enormous rubber plant and ashtrays on chrome stalks. Clara had sat there herself once, with her mother, waiting for an interview with the Head.

She walked along the corridor to her classroom, which was also quite empty, with thick gold bars of sunlight falling on the desks and a peaceful feeling, as though no one had been here for a long time nor ever would come. Clara opened the cupboard in the corner, took out one of the science overalls and put it on, and then sat down at her desk. After about a minute Mrs Mayhew came in carrying her clothes and her shoes. She said, 'I should put these on now, Clara,' and stood beside her while she did so. 'Would you like to go home?' she asked, and when Clara said that she wouldn't, thank you, Mrs Mayhew went on briskly, 'Right you are, then, Clara. You'd better get on with some homework, then, till the first period.'

All morning people kept coming up to her to say, 'Well done!' or just to pat her on the back. She was a celebrity right up till dinner time but after that it tailed off a bit. Half-way through the morning one of the prefects came in and told her the Head wanted to see her straight after school.

The Head's study was more like a sitting room, except for the big paper-strewn desk that she sat behind. She was busy writing when Clara came in: she just looked up to say, 'Hello, Clara. Sit down. Do you mind if I just finish these reports off? I won't be a minute.' She went on writing and Clara sat and looked at a photo of the Head's husband, who had square sensible-looking glasses, and her three boys who were all the same but different sizes. The Head slapped the pile of reports together and pushed her chair back. 'There . . . Well now . . . So what was all that about, this morning?'

'I don't know,' said Clara.

The Head looked at her, thoughtfully, and Clara looked back. Just before the silence became really embarrassing the Head said, 'I daresay you don't. Were you trying to attract attention?'

Clara considered. 'Well, I would, wouldn't I? Doing a thing like that. I mean – you'd be bound to.'

The Head nodded. 'Quite. Silly question.'

'Oh, no,' said Clara hastily. 'I meant you'd be bound to attract attention. Not be bound to be trying to.'

The Head asked, 'How do you feel about it now?'

Clara tried to examine her feelings, which slithered away like fish. In the end she said, 'I don't really feel anything,' which was, in a way, truthful.

The Head nodded again. 'Everything all right at home?'

'Oh, fine,' Clara assured her. 'Absolutely fine.'

'Good,' said the Head. 'Of course . . . I was just thinking, there are quite a lot of people in 4B with separated parents, aren't there? Bryony and Susie Tallance and Rachel.'

'And Midge,' said Clara. 'And Lucy Potter.'

'Yes. Five. Six, with you.'

'Twenty-five per cent,' said Clara. 'Just about.'

'Quite. As a matter of fact that's the national average, did you know? One marriage in four.'

'No, I didn't actually,' said Clara.

'Well, it is, I'm afraid. Anyway . . . You're not fussing about GCSEs, are you?'

'Not really,' said Clara. 'I mean, I don't like exams, but I don't mind as much as some people.'

'Your mocks were fine,' said the Head. 'Science could have been a bit better. But there shouldn't be any great problems there. So . . . Are you still going around with Liz Raymond?'

'Mostly,' said Clara. 'And Stephanie.'

'I want people to come and talk to me if there's anything they're worried about,' said the Head. 'Even things that may seem silly. You know. It doesn't have to be large obvious things. Exams and stuff. Anything.'

'Yes,' said Clara.

The phone rang. The Head picked it up and said no, she hadn't, and yes, she'd be along as soon as she could and tell them to wait. She put the receiver down and said, 'It wasn't like you, Clara, was it? I mean – there are a few people one wouldn't be *all* that surprised, if they suddenly did something idiotic or unexpected. But you aren't really like that, are you?'

Clara agreed that she wasn't, really.

'I'll be writing a note to your mother. And if you have an urge to do something like that again come and have a talk to me first, right?' The Head smiled and Clara smiled back. That was all, evidently. Clara got up and left. As she was closing the door she saw the Head looking after her, not smiling now, her expression rather bleak.

Most of the school had gone home but all those in Clara's class who had boyfriends at St. Benet's, which was practically everyone, were hanging around the bus station deliberately not catching buses because St Benet's came out half an hour later. Clara hung around for a bit too, just to be sociable, and then got on her bus. She sat on the top deck by herself and looked down onto the pavements. It was very hot; everyone young had bare legs, road menders were stripped to the waist, everywhere there was flesh – brown backs and white knees and glimpses of the hair under people's arms and the clefts between breasts and buttocks. In the park, the grass was strewn with sunbathers; there were girls in bikinis sprawled like starfish, face down with a rag of material between their legs and the strings of the top half undone. Clara, with no bra or pants on, could feel warm air washing around between her skin and her clothes. Coming down the stairs as the bus approached her stop, she had to hold down her skirt in case it blew up.

Her mother was already home. She worked part-time as a dentist's receptionist and had what were called flexible hours, which meant more or less that she worked when it suited her. Afternoons, nowadays, often didn't suit because Stan, her friend, who was an actor, was only free in the afternoons.

Stan wasn't there today though. Clara came into the kitchen where her mother was drinking tea and looking at a magazine. 'Hi!' she said. 'Any news?' which was what she said most days. Clara said that there was no news and her mother went on reading. Presently she yawned, pushed the magazine over to Clara and went upstairs to have a bath. Clara had another cup of tea and leafed through the magazine and then began to do her homework.

The Head's letter came a couple of days later. Clara heard the post flop onto the doormat and when she looked over the bannister she knew at once what the typed envelope must be. At the same moment Stan, who had stayed the night, came out of her mother's room on his way to the bathroom. He wore underpants and had a towel slung round his neck like a football scarf, and was humming to himself. When he saw her he said,

'Wotcha![1] How's tricks, then?' and Clara pulled her dressing gown more closely round her and said, 'Fine thanks.'

'That's the stuff,' said Stan vaguely. 'Hey – I got a couple of tickets for the show. Bring a friend, OK?' He was a stocky, muscular man with a lot of black hair on his chest. The smell of him, across the landing, was powerful – a huge inescapable wave of man smell: sweat and aftershave and something you could not put your finger on. Clara always knew when he was in the house before she opened the sitting room door because whiffs of him gusted about the place. She said, 'Thanks very much. That would be super,' and edged into her room.

When she came down they were both having breakfast. Her mother was just opening the post. She said, 'Coffee on the stove, lovely. Oh goody – my tax rebate's come.' She opened the Head's letter and began to read. First she stared at it with a puzzled look and then she began to laugh. She clapped her hand over her mouth, spluttering. 'I don't believe it!' she cried. 'Clara, I simply do not believe it! Stan just listen to this . . . isn't she the most incredible girl! Guess what she did! She took off all her clothes in school assembly and walked out starkers!' She handed the letter to Stan and went on laughing.

Stan read the letter. Grinning hugely, he looked up at Clara. 'She'll have done it for a dare, I bet. Good on yer, Clara. Terrific! God, I wish I'd been there!' He patted Clara's arm and Clara froze. She went completely rigid, as though she had turned to cement, and when eventually she moved a leg it seemed as though it should make a cracking noise.

Her mother had stopped laughing and was talking again. ' . . . the last thing anyone would have expected of you, lovey. You've always been such a prude. Ever since you were a toddler. Talk about modest! Honestly, Stan, she was hilarious, as a little kid – I can see her now, sitting on the beach at Camber clutching a towel round her in case anyone got a glimpse of her bum when she was changing. Aged 10. And when her bust

---

[1] **Wotcha**   an old-fashioned greeting meaning 'hi' or 'hello'

grew she used to sit hunched over like a spoon so no one would notice it. And if she had to strip off for the doctor you'd have thought that he'd been about to rape her, from her expression. Even now I can't get her out of that Victorian one-piece school regulation bathing costume – and it's not as though she's not got a good shape.'

'Smashing!' said Stan, slurping his coffee.

' . . . spot of puppy fat still but that's going, good hips, my legs if I may say so. Which is what makes this such an absolute scream. Honestly, sweetie, I wouldn't have thought you had it in you. I mean, I've not been allowed to see her in the buff myself since she was 12. Honestly, I've wondered once or twice if there was something wrong with the girl.' Her mother beamed across the breakfast table. 'Anyway, old Mrs Whatsit doesn't seem to be making a fuss. She just thinks I ought to know. More coffee, anyone? God, look at the time! And I said I'd be in early today . . . I'm off. Leave the breakfast things, lovey – we'll do them later. Coming Stan?'

Clara went on sitting at the table. She ate a piece of toast and drank her coffee. Her mother and Stan bustled about collecting her purse and his jacket and banged out of the house, shouting goodbye. The front gate clicked, the car door slammed, and then Clara began to cry, the tears dripping from her chin onto her folded arms and her face screwed up like a small child's.

Further reading

If you enjoyed *Clara's Day*, you might like to read more of Penelope Lively's short stories in *Pack of Cards* (Harper Perennial, 1990). Also entertaining are Roald Dahl's autobiographical works, *Boy: Tales of Childhood* (Puffin Books, 2001) and *Going Solo* (Puffin Books, 2001).

Sliding

by Leslie Norris

Leslie Norris was a teacher and head teacher until 1974 when he became a full-time writer. His stories, like this one, often deal with incidents from childhood that remain with us as adults.

The cold had begun very suddenly on Tuesday night, when Bernard had gone out to play. The boys were playing kick-the-tin in the lamplight at the top of the street, and nobody realized how cold it was until Randall Jenkins went home for his cap and scarf. Then they all felt the bitter weather – at their knees, their wrists, the tips of their ears. Bernard went indoors and borrowed his father's knitted scarf and found his own old gloves from last winter. Pretty soon, the game was on again and they forgot about the weather.

That night in bed, the sheets were hard and slippery, unfriendly as ice. Carefully, by an act of will, Bernard made warm a place in bed exactly the same shape as his body, thin and hunched under the covers. He extended it gradually, inch by inch, sending his toes gently into the cold until at last he was straight and comfortable. Everything was fine then, except that he had to pull the blankets firmly about his ears and shoulders. In the morning, the window was covered with frost flowers, and the kitchen fire blazed ferociously against the Welsh winter. He called for Danny Kenyon, as usual, on the way to school. Danny was his best friend, and they ran all the way, although Danny was short and plump.

Bernard was used now to the ice. Out in the yard, the tap had been frozen for days and a tongue of glass poked out of its mouth. Every morning was grey and spiteful, churlish light making the whole world dingy. Patches of hard grit gathered in the gutters and at the corners of streets, whipping against the boy's face and into his eyes. All day long, the shops kept their lights on, but there was nothing cheerful about them; only

Mr Toomey's shop was strong with colour, because of the brilliant globes of his pyramids of oranges.

In school on Friday morning, Albert Evans began to cry. The teacher asked him why, but Albert wouldn't answer. It was Randall Jenkins who told about Albert's legs. The inside of his thighs was chafed raw – red all the way from his groin to his knees. The skin was hard and angry, and there were weeping cracks in it. The teacher let Albert sit in front, near the stove, and he didn't have to do any arithmetic. When Bernard told his mother about Albert's legs, she narrowed her mouth and said that Annie Evans had no more sense than the day she was born, and then she took a pot of ointment over to Albert's house. While she was out, Bernard's father told him it had been the coldest day in more than twenty years. It was funny about skin and cold weather. Some boys turned red because of the cold, and some rather blue, and Danny Kenyon's knees went a kind of mottled colour – but he only laughed. When Bernard's mother came back, she was vexed. 'Poor little scamp' she said. 'It's agony for him to walk at all.'

After breakfast on Saturday morning, Bernard climbed into his den, which was the room above the stable in the yard. His father had whitewashed the walls for him, and together they'd carried up some old chairs from the house. Two large kitchen tables, covered with paints and bits of models and old newspapers, stood side by side under the windows. His record-player was there, too, and it was warm because of the oil stove. It was a fine room, with an enormous spider in the corner of the roof and a web thick and black against the white wall. Bernard sat in a chair near the stove and began to think of the things he would do when the summer came and he would be nine, going on ten. He and Danny Kenyon would go camping, they would find a field that nobody else knew about, and every day would be cloudless. He made the field in his head – the perfect green of its grass, its great protective tree in one corner, and its stream so pure that you could see every fragmentary pebble, every waving strand of weed in its bed. They were too young to go camping. He knew that.

And then Randall Jenkins climbed the stairs. He was grinning. He carried about his neck a pair of heavy boots, tied by their laces. He took them off and dropped them proudly on the floor, where they stood bluntly on their uncouth soles, exactly as if they still had someone's feet in them and invisible legs climbing up from them. Randall held out his hands to the stove and danced slowly around it, revolving so that he warmed himself all over.

'Coming sliding?' he said. 'This afternoon? We're all going – on the big pond; it's holding.'

'I'll ask,' said Bernard. 'I expect it will be all right.'

He thought of the big pond under the hills, its heavy acres hundreds of yards wide, the water cold and thick. It held in its silence fabulous pike, more than a yard long and twenty pounds in weight, although Bernard had never seen one. He didn't like the big pond.

'You'll need special boots,' said Randall. 'I've borrowed my brother's – take a look at them.'

He lifted the great boots and held them for Bernard's inspection. The soles were an inch thick and covered with a symmetrical pattern of bold nails – flat squares shining like silver. Crescents of smooth metal were screwed at heel and toe into the leather, the edges worn thin as a razor.

Randall rubbed his sleeve over the scarred toe caps, breathing on them as he burnished.

'These are the ones,' he said. 'My brother's old working boots. They might have been made for sliding.'

'They're too big for you,' said Bernard.

'Size 7,' said Randall with satisfaction. 'My brother's grown out of them. Three or four pairs of socks and they'll fit me – you watch, I'll scream right across the pond.'

He moved the boots through the air as if they were fighter planes.

'You'll need a pair like this,' he said. 'Otherwise you'll never go any distance.'

Randall was lucky to have big brothers. Bernard thought dismally of his own boots – light, gentlemanly, with rubber soles and heels. His grandfather didn't like rubber soles and heels, either. Only thieves and policemen, he had said, two classes of society with much in common, wear rubber on their feet. Bernard didn't understand that.

'Is Danny Kenyon coming?' Bernard asked.

'Sure,' Randall said. 'We're all going. I told you.'

After lunch, they all went to the pond, protected by layers of clothing against the wind's knives, their woollen hats pulled over their ears. Some of the boys had managed to borrow heavy boots, just to be like Randall Jenkins, and they clumped awkwardly up the hill as they learned to manage their erratic feet. Randall Jenkins turned out his toes, shuffling around corners like Charlie Chaplin, and they all laughed.

Bernard began to feel very happy. He began to imagine the long quietness of his gliding over the ice. He thought of thick ice, clear as glass, beneath which the cold fish swam, staring up with their goggle eyes at the sliding boys. He thought of ice like a dazzling mirror set in the hills, on which they could skim above their own images, each brilliant slider like two perfect boys – one upside down – joined at the feet. In his happiness he jostled and bumped against Danny Kenyon, and Danny charged right back at him, until they were both laughing and the wind blew away their white breath in clouds from their mouths.

But the pond was a disappointment. Winter had taken all the life from the hills, and the face of the ice was grey and blind – the colour of the flat sky above it. There were no reeds at the lake's edge. Featureless, the ice stretched on, swept by an unhindered wind. The boys bent their heads down against the brutal cold. Their voices were feeble; they felt small and helpless. Only Randall Jenkins was unaffected. Whooping and waving at the ice, he began to run, lifting his enormous boots in slow, high-stepping strides. He ran on, planting his laughable feet one after the other so heavily that Bernard imagined he could hear the whole bowl ringing; and then, his legs rigid, both arms raised for balance, he slid with comic dignity. They all rushed after him, sliding and calling. The afternoon was suddenly warm and vigorous.

Bernard was a good runner, and he hurled himself along so that the momentum of his first slide would be memorable. He raced past two or three of the boys and then stopped, his legs braced wide, head up, arms raised. He was expecting something birdlike, something approaching flight, but nothing happened. His rubber soles clung wickedly to the surface of the ice and he slid no more than a few yards. He was inconsolable.

He shuffled cautiously along the margins of the ice, tentative and humble. Far out, in the wide middle of the pond, he could see the dark figures of his friends, freely sliding, gyrating, crouching, skating on one leg. Their voices came bouncing to him high and clear like the calling of seagulls. But he ran alone at the edge of the lake, unable to slide. Then, unexpectedly, without warning, he found himself free of the binding friction that had held him. He had begun to glide. He sat on the bank, lifted one foot, and inspected the sole of his boot. A thin layer of polished ice, thinner than a postage stamp, had built itself onto the black rubber. He saw that the other boot was also transformed, and he ran jubilantly into the heart of the pond, far outstripping the loud boys, sliding far and fast, hearing their admiration and surprise. The pond was his.

Late in the afternoon came two young men, tall, with deep voices, all of seventeen years old. They strapped on their sharp and proper skates, and skated expertly. Briefly, the boys watched them, but soon Randall Jenkins had organised a game of follow-my-leader. Randall was a superb leader, his invention and audacity encouraging them to a skill and daring they had not known they possessed. The last dare was to run as fast as they could toward the ice from the shore itself, leaping from the bank at full speed. Randall raced forward, his long slow legs gathering pace as he ran, and then he leaped high outward from the bank, landing yards out. Rigid as a scarecrow, he sped on, stopping at last a prodigious way out, and standing absolutely still in the attitude of his sliding. One by one they followed him, although nobody was as brave as Randall, nobody would hurl himself as uninhibitedly from the steep bank. At last, only three boys were left. Bernard thought he had never seen anything as lovely as the dark ice, hardly lit at all as the light faded, and the still figures of his friends dotted about on it, not moving, their arms in a variety of postures, their bodies bent or upright. He took a great breath, and ran. He had never felt so light, he was full of fiery energy. He reached the bank and thrust himself so urgently, so powerfully, that the exhilaration of his leap made him gasp. He hit the ice beautifully, and felt at once the speed of his sliding, and he knew that nobody had ever slid so far. Stopping at last, he looked around. He was yards farther than Randall Jenkins, miles farther than the other boys. Jackie Phelps was slowing miserably a long way off, and only Danny was left to jump.

He could see Danny up on the bank, preparing to run, swaying from one foot to the other, bent forward at the waist. Cupping his hands, Bernard shouted, 'You'll never reach me!'

Danny waved furiously. You could see that he was going to give it all he had by the way he set his shoulders. He ran forward and leaped wildly from the bank. Bernard could see him so clearly that everything seemed to happen in slow motion. He saw Danny hit the ice and knew that it was wrong. Danny landed on his heels, not on the flat of his feet, and his body was already tilting gently backward. He sped along, the slope of his body already irrevocably past the point of recovery. They saw his heels leave the ice, and for a perceptible moment he sailed through the unsupporting air before the back of his head cracked frighteningly against the surface. He lay broken and huddled. Bernard could not move. He could see Danny in a black heap, but he couldn't move toward him. It was Randall Jenkins who reached him first, and they all ran in behind him.

They crowded around Danny, looking down at him. His face was still and white, his eyes closed. As they looked, a little worm of blood appeared at one nostril and curled onto Danny's lip. What if he should die? Bernard bent, and in an urgency of terror lifted his friend. Randall helped him, and together they hauled Danny to the bank. Some of the boys were crying, and Randall set them to collect twigs, pieces of paper – anything that would burn. Bernard took off Danny's gloves and rubbed his hands in his own. Danny's fingers were very cold, but in a while he began to move and groan. Twice he opened his eyes, without recognising them and without saying anything. Randall lit a fire, and it burned with a dull light, sullenly. He sent all the boys except Bernard to find more fuel, told them to rip branches from small trees. Bernard wiped the blood from Danny's nose, and after a while the bleeding stopped. It hadn't been very much, he comforted himself. His knees hurt from bending down so long. Behind him, Randall had whipped the fire into a huge blaze that pushed away the darkness, and the boys sat near it, not speaking. Danny moved heavily, sat up, and looked at Bernard.

'Oh, my God,' said Danny Kenyon. 'What happened?'

He was all right; everything was all right. The boys cheered, slapped each other on the back, put Danny to sit even nearer the fire. They danced and sang, released from fright, and they were pert and arrogant when one of the young men suddenly appeared.

'What's the matter with him?' he asked, bending over Danny.

'Nothing,' said Randall airily. 'Nothing at all.'

'None of your business,' said Jackie Phelps, out of the darkness.

'How old are you?' said the young man to Bernard.

'Ten,' lied Bernard. He pointed to Randall. 'And he's eleven,' he said.

'Get that boy home,' said the young man. 'How do you feel, son?'

'Great,' said Danny. 'I feel great.'

'Get home,' said the young man. 'And the rest of you see that this fire is out.'

He skated into the darkness. Bernard could feel the iron shearing of his blades.

The fire was very hot. Bernard could imagine it warming a thin crust of frozen soil, then maybe deeper, a half inch deep. Already he could hear the ice hiss in the released ground. He sat with his back up against Danny's back, so they were both comfortable. All the boys sat around. They were very quiet.

Bit by bit, the dark and the cold crept into the interstices of the flames, winning the night back for winter. Randall got up and stamped about. His feet had gone to sleep.

'Time to go, lads,' he said. 'Time to go.'

They stood up and followed obediently behind Randall. Bernard was so tired that his legs were slow and stiff, and his mind was always about two steps in front of them, but in a little while they got better. The boys went down the lane past the old rectory and started down the hill toward the town. A night wind flew at them as if it cared nothing for people and meant to blow straight through them. Bernard began to shiver. What if Danny had died? He saw again Danny's face as he lay on the ice, as white and stiff as a candle. As he looked, an imaginary worm of blood crawled from Danny's nose and covered the side of his cheek. He closed his mind from the terror of it and put his arm over Danny's shoulder.

'How do you feel?' he whispered, but Randall heard him.

'He feels great,' Randall Jenkins roared, his voice red as fire. 'What's the matter with you? He feels fine!'

'I'm OK,' said Danny. 'Honest, I'm OK.'

A few small flakes of snow fell out of the sky. The boys felt them hit their faces, light as cobwebs, and then vanish. It was intolerably dark and cold. As they entered the first streets of the town, the boys moved together for solace[1] and started to run. They trotted close together, moving home as one boy through the darkness, united against whatever terror might threaten them.

---

[1]**solace**   comfort in times of sadness

Further reading

Leslie Norris's short stories are collected in *The Girl from Cardigan: Sixteen Stories* (Gibbs Smith, 1988). You might also enjoy the short stories of David Almond in *Counting Stars* (Hodder Children's Books, 2007).

Taming the Tiger

by Tony Anthony

Tony Anthony is a three-times World Kung Fu champion. His auto-biography, *Taming the Tiger,* tells how at the height of his success he lost direction in his life and turned into a bloodthirsty, violent man. This extract tells us about his childhood.

I was four years old when the stranger arrived. People didn't come to our house, so when the doorbell rang I stood excitedly at the top of the stairs. My father let him in and showed him through to the living room. The stranger was Chinese, like my mother. I crept down to take a peek through the half-open door. They were talking in such low voices I couldn't make out what they were saying. From my hiding place, I could see the stranger's face. It was mean looking.

'Come in, Antonio.' Mum's voice startled me. Being careful not to look directly at the man, I pushed quickly past him and tried to hide behind my father's legs. Mum reached out and pulled me to her. I didn't know what to do. I looked to Dad, but he just stared at the fireplace. He was blinking heavily, as though he had something stuck in his eye.

Suddenly, the stranger took me by the wrist. Flinching, I tried to pull away, but he held me tightly and Mum gave me that look, the one she used when I was to be quiet. She handed the stranger a small bag and, almost before I knew it, we were outside, walking down our garden path, leaving my parents behind.

I don't remember much about the journey. The stranger said nothing to me. I had no idea where he was taking me. When I found myself at the airport I began to tingle with a mixture of excitement and fear. This might be a fantastic adventure, but no, something was wrong, really wrong. The stranger still did not speak as we started to board a plane. As time passed, I grew more and more fearful. It seemed the flight was never going to end. Surely Mum and Dad would come soon? We'd go back to the house. Everything would be alright. Little did I know, I was on a plane bound for China.

At four years old I couldn't have understood the complexities of my parents' lives. What I did know, however, was my mother's hatred. Sitting on the plane, all I could do was think of her being angry with me. What had I done this time? I knew I had ruined my mother's life. She told me so. She was always angry.

Some time before the stranger came there was an incident I have never forgotten. We had moved from our little West End flat into a big house in Edgware, north-west London. To me it seemed huge and I remember squealing excitedly, running from one room to another. Mum and Dad bought a big new bed and I was bouncing on it, throwing myself face first into the soft new duvet. Suddenly Mum came storming in. 'Stop that immediately, you stupid child!' she yelled, dealing me a harsh slap across my legs. Moving over to the dressing table, she picked up the large hand mirror and started to look at herself, jutting out her chin, poking her lips and preening her eyelashes in the way she always did. I scrambled to quickly get off the bed but, in my haste, missed my footing and came bouncing down into the quilt once more. I couldn't help but let out a gasp of laughter.

Before I knew it, she was upon me. There was crashing around my head, an almighty cracking noise and my mother's voice, shrill, swearing and cursing at me. My head swam with sudden, intense pain.

'You idiot child, what did I tell you?' she was screaming in a frenzy. 'Now look at you!'

She marched out of the room slamming the door behind her. Somehow, I couldn't move. The frame of the mirror stuck tight over my shoulders and pointed razors of glass were cutting into my neck and face. There was blood too, and more came as I winced in agony, willing myself to pull a sharp edge away from my cheek.

I awoke with a start and realised we were getting off the plane. Where were we? I tried to rub my eyes, but the stranger still held my wrist. I wanted to cry. There was a lot of chatter, but I couldn't understand any of it. People were shouting, but their voices were high-pitched and peculiar. Fear and confusion swept over me. Who was this man? Where had he brought me? People scurried around with bags, trolleys and parcels, but it wasn't like the airport we had been in at the beginning of the journey. The air was thick with cigarette smoke and other strange smells. Overwhelmed with drowsiness, I began to cry, in big, breathless sobs. 'Sshh!' demanded the stranger, sharply tightening his grip so I felt his fingernails in my flesh. My wailing was quickly suppressed in pain and silent terror. He tugged again, this time pulling me out into the evening air. It was then I realised I was far, very far, from home.

Like a frightened rabbit, I scanned the scene, hoping to catch sight of my mother or father. The people wore strange clothes. There was a lot of shouting and dogs barking and a man with birds in a cage. We stopped. Before me stood a spindly man dressed in a silky black jacket with wide, loose sleeves and a high collar. Later, I learned this was my grandfather. At the time, there was no introduction. No smile. No welcome. I was hoisted roughly onto his horse-drawn cart and, at the click of his tongue, we pulled away into the night.

As we left the airport behind I could see strange-shaped shadows of trees and animals moving around in the half-light. I was terrified and felt queasy with the stink that filled the air. (I was later to discover that it was the lily soap my grandfather used. It is very common among the Chinese, renowned for its antiseptic properties, but its odious perfume has always sickened my stomach.) It was to become the scent of my paranoia.

The journey seemed never-ending. When we finally came to a standstill it was pitch black. I could barely make out the shadowy surroundings, but I sensed there was a group of women standing at a gateway. Perhaps they were waiting for us. The women didn't like me. I felt that instantly. But what had I done wrong? My mind kept flashing back to my mother. Then, with looks of disdain and a crow-like cackle, the women were gone, all except one. She was 'Jowmo', my grandmother.

Inside the house I shivered with cold. Still no one spoke to me. I wanted to ask where I was, but when I tried to speak I was met with a finger to the lips and a harsh 'Shush!' I was 4 years old and completely alone in a hostile, frightening world.

The house was very strange. I was shocked when suddenly a whole wall moved. The woman ushered me towards the bed in the corner. It looked nothing like my bed at home. Sticks of bamboo lay over a rickety frame. It creaked as I climbed onto it and pinched my skin when I moved. The thin muslin sheet barely covered me, but I tucked it round my shoulders, pulled my knees up to my chest and wept silently until sleep came. In the days and weeks ahead I quickly learned to stem my tears.

Each day began very early, around 4 or 5 o'clock. My grand-father (Lowsi, as I was instructed to call him, meaning 'master' or 'teacher') came into my room and beat me about the head with his bamboo stick to wake me. Soon I was rising before I heard his footsteps. I made sure I was up and ready to greet him. He hit me anyway. Lowsi's beatings were brutal. In the days and weeks ahead I got used to them, but they were always hard to bear. He used fresh bamboo cane, striking me over my ears, often until I bled. There was rarely any explana-tion or reason. He branded me *Lo han quilo*, meaning 'Little foreign devil'. It was his personal quest to 'beat the round-eye out of me'.

As my grandparents' only male grandchild, I might have been treated very differently. Boys in China are considered to bring good fortune and honour to a family and are often referred to as 'little emperors'. They are spoilt and doted upon[1] by parents and, even more so, by grandparents. The problem was that my mother had married an outsider, an Italian, who was born and bred in England. She had brought shame on the family. It seemed I was to pay for the profanity.[2]

---

[1]**doted upon**   given special treatment
[2]**profanity**   (in this context) bad behaviour

Each morning I dutifully followed Lowsi out to the court-yard where he began his morning exercises. For several hours I shivered in my thin muslin robe but I hardly dared take my eyes off him, for fear of being beaten again. Sometimes I stole a glance up to the roof and the tops of the walls. They were decorated with the most bizarre things: dragons, phoenix, flying horses, unicorns and a man riding a hen.

At first, I could only watch as Lowsi performed his strange movements. He made me stand very still and breathe deeply, in through my nose and out through my mouth. It was mind-numbingly tedious. As the weeks went by, and I began to pick up his language, he explained that his moves were 'Tai Chi', a discipline that is fundamental to the way of Kung Fu.

I quickly gathered that my grandfather was a Grand Master in the ancient martial art. He was revered by everyone in the village. That was why our house was grander than any of the others. I thought it looked a bit like the temple up on the hill.

Detail of my family tree is somewhat sparse in my mind, but I know that my grandfather originated from northern China. He fled down to Canton to escape the torturous atrocities of the Japanese invasion that extended into the 1940s. He was born into the Soo family, a direct descendant of Gong Soo, one of the so-called 'Venerable Five', who escaped the destruction of the original Shaolin temple under the Manchu dynasty in 1768. Gong Soo went into hiding and continued to practise Kung Fu. His knowledge passed down from generation to generation until my grandfather, Cheung Ling Soo.

As a Shaolin monk, my grandfather was proud of this 500-year-long heritage. Leaving the temple of his training, he began to develop his own styles and teach the ways of Kung Fu. He soon became a highly honoured Grand Master. Having no son of his own, however, meant the Soo lineage would be broken. I was his most unexpected and unlikely disciple. Perhaps it was for this reason that he would drive me to the harshest extremes of training. As part 'round-eye', he knew I would have much to prove. In the years ahead, Lowsi would reveal to me the secrets and treasures of the ancient art. I would become a highly disciplined, truly enlightened disciple and an unbeatable combat warrior.

Further reading

A number of writers tell about their roller-coaster lives in their autobiographies. You could try Sharon Osbourne's *Extreme: My Autobiography* (Time Warner Paperbacks, 2006). If you would prefer a gripping sporting autobiography, try *The Crossing: Conquering the Atlantic in the World's Toughest Rowing Race* by James Cracknell and Ben Fogle (Atlantic Books, 2006).

I Wish I Were . . .

by Rabindranath Tagore

> Rabindranath Tagore was a poet and philosopher from Bengal who won the Nobel Prize in literature in 1913. In this poem he reflects on the fact that, as children, all of us have ambitions as to who we would like to become.

When the gong sounds ten in the morning and I walk to
    school by our lane,
Every day I meet the hawker[1] crying, 'Bangles, crystal
    bangles?'
There is nothing to hurry him on, there is no road he must
    take, no place he must go to, no time when he must come
    home.
I wish I were a hawker, spending my day in the road, crying
    'Bangles, crystal bangles!'

---

[1]**hawker**   someone who travels around selling things

When at four in the afternoon I come back from the school,
I can see through the gate of that house the gardener digging
the ground.
He does what he likes with his spade, he soils his clothes with
dust,
Nobody takes him to task if he gets baked in the sun or gets wet.
I wish I were a gardener digging away at the garden with
nobody to stop me from digging.
Just as it gets dark in the evening and my mother sends me to
bed,
I can see through the open window the watchman walking up
and down.
The lane is dark and lonely, and the street-lamp stands like a
giant with one red eye in its head.
The watchman² swings his lantern and walks with his shadow
at his side, and never once goes to bed in his life.
I wish I were a watchman walking the streets all night, chasing
the shadows with my lantern.

²**watchman**   in the past, someone paid to keep watch in a town at night

Further reading

You may wish to explore more of Rabindranath Tagore's poems in *Selected Poems* (Penguin Books Ltd, 2005). If you enjoy reading about what it is like to grow up in another country, try *Oleander, Jacaranda* by Penelope Lively (Penguin Books Ltd, 2006), in which the author describes her upbringing in Egypt and reflects on what it means to be British.

I Was Left with a Childcarer . . . and Never Collected

by Barbara Brown

This is the first of a number of texts that show how people cope in difficult situations. Barbara Brown's article for *The Guardian* looks back at a disturbing event in her childhood and at how it shaped the rest of her life.

My children, all now with families of their own, seem to think my growing-up days were unique. So here goes. In 1933, when I was 16 months old, my mother dropped me off as a day baby with a carer, in Kilburn, north-west London, promised to pick me up at half past five, and then disappeared. The old lady, who took in so many young charges, did not know that my mother, unlike all the others, was never to collect me later in the day.

The dim three-storey house in Loveridge Road became my home. The house was always bare of furniture – bare floors, gaslights with no shades, the old armchair full of mice. My little bed was two old armchairs pushed together, and my bedding one blanket and some old 1914 greatcoats. I can still feel those huge army buttons hitting me in the teeth as I pulled them up around me on a cold night.

The house was full of mice, even though we had a cat, and the prints on the wall housed the bugs, which crawled out at night. The place smelled of a mixture of suet puddings, brown ale and tobacco.

My foster mum, however, was wonderful. But by the age of 12, I was nursing her. She had frequent bouts of night cramp and I would have to walk her about in the early hours to ease her pain. I would cut her toenails, rub her back with liniment, clean her ears out, light the range and do the housework – and all this before school. By then I had long learned to cook a meal. When I look back, I realise what a scruffy kid I was, in my funny old second-hand clothes. Such things were not important in our house; what has stayed with me is that ours was a home of laughter and cuddles.

When the war began, our vicar asked if I would like to go to the country. I declined, saying that if my mum were to die in the bombing, I would die with her. Each night as the bombs dropped, Mum and I sat under the stairs with the cat and the coal, singing all the songs from the Edwardian era. I knew them all.

But I had become a terrible liar. I was always inventing stories about myself. I used to say I had a mum who was beautiful, with lovely hair and eyes, and she couldn't look after me because she was a mannequin,[1] and busy working. I made a little world of my own, and it helped me to cope.

As I grew into adulthood and began to see for myself the sadness and poverty that had surrounded me, I tried in a feeble way to improve my situation. I bought myself nice soap, new shoes, treats to eat for tea. I began to complain about the house and the bleakness of it. I had been reading the works of Dickens and could see in them the reality of my own upbringing.

In 1952 I met Ron through *Picture Post* magazine; it used to have a page of penfriends. He was a serviceman and we wrote to each other over a couple of years, but I was afraid that if he saw the conditions of our home, he wouldn't bother with me again. I knew it was best he never saw where I lived. To my horror, he did one time visit the house, unannounced. I opened the door with curlers in my hair, and dirty knees from scrubbing the floor. He said, 'Hello, does Barbara live here?' I said, 'That's me.'

My fears were unfounded – he liked my foster parents, and he liked me. Within two years we were married. I borrowed my friend's wedding dress, and another lent me a veil and a pearl necklace. My foster parents, by then in their 80s, turned up in a neighbour's car, my foster mother in a long coat and plimsolls. Indeed, my own mother showed up. I wish now that I had asked her so many questions, but she seemed so hard and

---

[1]**mannequin**   someone employed to display clothes to customers

unapproachable – we were really like strangers. Much later, when I gave birth to my own daughter, I found out where she lived and turned up on her doorstep, but she wouldn't let us in.

By that time I had said goodbye to the house in Kilburn, and felt no pangs at doing so. But with all the comforts I now have, I still look back on those early days and kind of miss them. Perhaps now I've got too much.

Further reading

Every Saturday, *Weekend* magazine (in *The Guardian*) runs an article called 'Experience', written by readers. They are always fascinating and emotional pieces. For an account of someone growing up in wartime, see *Worlds Apart: A Wartime Childhood Odyssey* by Janet Buchanan-Wilson (DRP, 2004).

Activities

Clara's Day

Before you read

1   During your school life you will attend hundreds of school assemblies. Which stick in your mind the most, and why? Discuss your ideas in a small group.

What's it about?

Read the story and answer questions 2 and 3 by yourself. Then compare your answers with a partner's.

2   Look again at the first sentence of the story. Choose the word you think best describes it:
    shocking   *funny*   *matter-of-fact*   *surprising*   *clever*

    Write a sentence or two to explain your choice.

3   Look again at the scene where Clara's mother reads out the letter from the headmistress. When her mother and Stan have left the house, Clara starts to cry. Interview Clara about what has happened in the story, why she took her clothes off in assembly, and how she feels now.

Thinking about the text

4   Which of these statements do you think best sums up the story?
    a   It shows the effects of divorce and separation.
    b   It shows how emotional teenage life can be.
    c   It shows how teenagers try to grab attention.
    d   It shows how emotions can affect the way we behave.
    e   It shows how difficult it is to cope with loneliness.

    Write a sentence to explain your choice.

5   Read Clara's interview with the headmistress again (from 'The Head's study was more like a sitting room' to 'her expression rather bleak'). Look particularly at the dialogue between the two characters. What is the Head's attitude towards Clara and her behaviour in assembly? What does she say that makes you think this? How does she say it? How does the Head's treatment of her make Clara feel? Write a paragraph or two explaining whether you think the Head has dealt with the situation adequately.

Sliding

Before you read

1   This story is about an accident in childhood. Think back to a time when you hurt yourself – for example, falling off your bike, tripping up, breaking your arm. Talk to a partner about what happened.

What's it about?

2   The story is told through the eyes of Bernard. Read the story and, using a chart or spider diagram, note down what we learn about him. For example, what is his background? What is his character?

3   Re-read the section that describes Danny's accident (from 'He could see Danny up on the bank' to 'they all ran in behind him'). What hints can you find that something is about to go wrong? What words and phrases does the author use to convey Bernard's feeling that something bad is going to happen (foreboding)? Write a paragraph or two explaining how effective you think the description of the accident is.

Thinking about the text

4   Look at the final paragraph of the story. Why do the boys react as they do, moving together 'for solace', so that they feel 'united against whatever terror might threaten them'? What are they afraid of? What do you think the boys have learned from their experience? Discuss your ideas in a small group.

5   Imagine that Bernard's mother asks him what he did when he went off on his own during the holiday. What would he say? How would he explain the events in the story? Are there any details he would keep to himself? Working in pairs, role-play the conversation. Think about:
   ● what happened
   ● the other people involved and what might have happened to them since then
   ● how the incident affected Bernard.

Taming the Tiger

Before you read

1   As young children, we all seem to have things that terrify us – creatures from films or stories, perhaps, or the fear of burglars or getting lost. Think back to your own childhood. What were the themes of your own nightmares and fears? Discuss one especially vivid fear you had as a child with a partner.

What's it about?

Read the extract and answer questions 2 to 4 by yourself. Then discuss your ideas in a small group.

2   In the opening sequence of this text, how does the writer convey the sense of confusion and menace he felt as a child? Which words and phrases particularly highlight these feelings? Write a paragraph explaining what you notice.

3   This text is in three sections. For each section write down:
   ● what happens
   ● what we learn about Tony Anthony

   How has Tony Anthony's character changed by the final section?

4   The author's first impression of China is that it is a frightening, confusing place which is very different from home. Using two columns, make a list to show what life is like for him at home and how it is different in China.

Thinking about the text

5   What overall impression do you get of Tony Anthony from the extract? Write a paragraph or two describing what he is like, both as a child and as the older writer looking back.

6   This extract would make a good film. Use description (e.g. 'At first the screen shows darkness. Then a door opens. We hear whispers . . . ') and dialogue (e.g. 'Mother? Mother is that you?') to write an exciting opening scene for a movie version of the text.

I Wish I Were . . .

Before you read

1   The first part of this text describes a journey to school. Think back
    to the first school you attended. How much can you remember of
    your first day there, and your journey to and from school?
    a   Draw a 60-second sketch of the things you remember.
    b   Interview a partner about his or her memories of school. Using
        his or her sketch as a starting point, find out as much as pos-
        sible about what he or she remembers.

    Share your findings with the rest of your class.

What's it about?

Read the poem and answer questions 2 and 3 by yourself. Then discuss your ideas in a small group.

2   The poem is set in India. What clues can you find in the poem
    about the setting?

3   What impression do you get of the poem's narrator? What age do
    you think he is? What is his character? Use a spider diagram to
    organise your thoughts.

Thinking about the text

4   What is it about the three jobs described in the poem that appeal
    to the narrator? What language does the poet use to convey this?
    Think about:
    ●   the effect of the repeated use of negatives ('nothing', 'no',
        'nobody' and 'never') in the description of the hawker's life
        (line 3), the gardener's life (lines 8–9) and the watchman's life
        (line 13)
    ●   the imagery used in the description of the street-lamp ('like a
        giant with one red eye in its head' (line 12)) and the watchman's
        life ('chasing the shadows' (line 14)).

    Discuss your ideas with others in your class.

5   Write your own poem called *I Wish I Were . . .* Structure your poem
    in three sections, like Rabindranath Tagore's, with each section
    dealing with a different time of day; alternatively, devise a structure
    of your own.

I Was Left with a Childcarer . . . and Never Collected

Before you read

1   Reality television and some magazine articles encourage people to speak or write openly about things that, in the past, they might have chosen to keep quiet about. Hold a class debate about whether it is a good idea to speak or write about personal matters in public. What are the arguments for and against doing so? In particular, does sharing the problems of our childhood help us to come to terms with those problems?

What's it about?

Read the story and answer questions 2 and 3 by yourself. Then discuss your answers in a small group.

2   Create a table to show what we learn about Barbara Brown from the article. Include facts about:
   ● where she lived as a child
   ● what her foster mother was like
   ● her relationship with Ron
   ● the different sides of her character.

3   Imagine a conversation between Barbara Brown and a friend in which the friend asks Barbara to imagine what her life would have been like if she hadn't been abandoned. What has she learned? How has the experience affected her? Think about what questions the friend might ask and how Barbara might answer them, then role-play the conversation.

Thinking about the text

4   When we think back to our childhood, we often see pictures, hear sounds, and remember smells. These help to bring memories to life. Which of the senses (sight, smell, touch, taste and sound) does Barbara Brown use in her article to evoke memories of her childhood? Write down at least three examples and say what effect they had on you.

5   What did you like and not like about Barbara Brown's article? Discuss your ideas in a small group. Use these questions to help you:
   ● What did you learn about Barbara Brown's life?
   ● What did you like about her account?
   ● How might the article have been improved?

Compare and contrast

1   What impressions of childhood do the different texts give? Write a sentence explaining which text is:

   a   the happiest

   b   the bleakest (most unhappy)

   c   the most different from your own life.

   Give a reason for each of your answers.

2   Choose two texts that you particularly enjoyed reading and write a short essay comparing them. Use these questions to help you:

   - What are the two texts about?
   - What are the main characters like?
   - How are the texts similar and how are they different?
   - What do you notice about the language used in each text?

3   Working in a small group, devise a chat show with the characters or authors from two or more of the texts in this section. For example, one might be Clara and another Rabindranath Tagore. Write a script in which the chat show host interviews the characters/authors about the best and worst times of childhood. Try to ask open questions (how? and why?) which encourage your guests to give developed answers rather than just saying 'yes' or 'no'. Perform your chat show for the rest of your class.

4   Imagine a television documentary about childhood in which the presenters are Clara from *Clara's Day*, Tony Anthony and one other character or author from the texts in this section. Each one has been asked to make a one-minute film which sums up their memories of their early childhood (e.g. life at school). Think about what each person's mini-documentary might contain – what images, what people, what words (spoken in voice-over or direct to camera)? Working in a small group, put together the mini-documentaries, showing the different views of each person.

2 Letting go

This section is about growing up and gaining independence. When we are very young, we often long to be more independent of the adults around us. When we get older, we sometimes wish life was simpler – as it seemed to be when we were children. The texts in this section cover a range of related themes – the teachers who influence us, the shift from innocence to experience, and the advice we need to make our own way in the world.

Activities

1   Think back to when you first started to show some independence from your parent(s) or carer(s). Was it when you first started seeing friends, or maybe an adventure with a friend on your bike? Write a paragraph describing how it felt to be independent of the adults in your life for the first time.

2   Adults often like to give advice to younger people – whether one-to-one or in assemblies or Citizenship lessons. Write a paragraph about the best and worst advice you have received in your life. Who did it come from? What was the situation? How did you react to the advice?

3   What advice would you give parents about how to deal with their children? How should they talk to them? How strict should they be? Devise a role play in which a child has done something wrong and is being reprimanded by his or her parent(s). Perhaps the child has stayed out too late and is being told off when he or she finally gets home. Create two versions – the first showing how *not* to do it (with the parent(s) shouting, being sarcastic and so on), the second showing how it should be done.

My Best Teacher

by Vic Reeves

A television commercial to recruit teachers used to say: 'No one forgets a good teacher.' Many of us have memories of teachers who have influenced us, building our confidence, teaching us skills and shifting our learning into new, undiscovered areas.

Each week *The Times Educational Supplement*, a newspaper aimed at teachers, asks a well-known person to think back to a teacher who influenced her or him. In this article it is the comedian Vic Reeves.

Mr Hodgson was quite cool. He was my English teacher at Eastbourne secondary, County Durham, from when I was 12 to 14 years old. With his long black hair and black beard, he looked a bit like Robert Wyatt, the drummer and singer in [Sixties rock band] Soft Machine.

He wore grey trousers, a cardigan, a checked shirt and specs – solid horn-rimmed black specs that matched his beard and hair. It's difficult to judge age when you're young, but I would have said he was in his 30s. He had polio. His grey trousers hid his twisted legs, and the clumpy shoes, I presume, housed his misshapen feet. Not that he appeared odd. To us kids, he was an ordinary bloke in a wheelchair.

When I think of him I see him smiling, and manoeuvring his wheelchair round our desks. I used to help him in and out of it, and sometimes in and out of his blue invalid car. I think he smoked a pipe; I quite liked the smell of Old Bruno, or whatever it was called. I knew nothing about his family, or even whether he had one. He was just a great bloke that I kind of had an affinity[1] with.

I was always well behaved in his class. I was on my best behaviour because I wanted to learn from him and do well. In maths and science, I couldn't care less. I'd spend most of my time entertaining my peers, pulling faces and drawing sketches of bottoms.

---

[1]**affinity**   something in common

Mr Hodgson used to make us really enthusiastic about English. We would read books like *Catcher in the Rye* and *Of Mice and Men*. He'd choose a paragraph or phrase and then talk about it with us. He'd make us interested in what was going on in the books by getting us to read out our favourite passage. He was good at making us appreciate words and how and where to use them.

Mr Hodgson suggested books for us to read that weren't on the curriculum. He'd find out what our interests were and suggest something we might like. I think he may have suggested I read *White Fang* by Jack London. I read it and loved it.

He had a good sense of humour, and was very kind and patient. He'd spend quarter of an hour with me at breaktime rather than go and have a coffee. He'd sit and talk to me about *New Musical Express*. He became a friend.

It started when I saw a copy on his desk and thought: 'That's cool. A teacher who's got the *NME*. I get that.' We had a rapport and shared similar musical tastes. It was a mutual appreciation society. He seemed as pleased to talk to me as I was to him. We didn't talk after school, though. Once the bell rang, I was off.

Eastbourne secondary was incredibly austere with high Victorian walls and huge windows. Rumour had it that at one time it had been a hospital for the terminally ill. Or a mental asylum. No one really knows. But it was grim. I didn't enjoy being there. I learnt a lot more when I was out of school, from my family.

My dad, Neill, had a huge vocabulary so I used to just listen to him. He spoke in an almost Dickensian[2] way. His father, Grampy, was a great educationalist. Whenever we visited, I was summoned to his study where he'd get out this huge leather dictionary. I'd close my eyes and pick a word before reading aloud its definition. Next time we visited I'd have to use it in some sort of context or conversation to prove I'd learnt its meaning.

---

[2]**Dickensian**   like a character in a Charles Dickens novel, some of whom speak in a quirky, long-winded way

I'd often find myself in Mr Hodgson's class thinking: 'How can I show off this new word I've learnt?' I always got good marks in English and was good at storytelling. Sometimes I'd make up stories about bands I'd seen. My lessons with him merged with my interest in words, art and music. He was part of the jigsaw that has made me who I am. I still read constantly.

None of us knew that he was dying. We were all called into assembly one day when the headmaster announced that he had died. I was 14 and it was such a shock. I cried. The whole school was upset. English wasn't the same after that.

Further reading

The Times Educational Supplement runs a weekly feature in which celebrities remember a teacher who influenced them. The newspaper is published every Friday. Laurie Lee's *Cider with Rosie* also contains humorous descriptions of teachers – especially the appalling 'Miss Crabby' (Vintage, 2002).

The Secret Life of Snap Decisions
by Malcolm Gladwell

This is an unusual text about how we human beings work. Malcolm Gladwell has written a book called *Blink* in which he explores why it is that our instant reactions to something or someone are so often correct. We meet someone for the first time and immediately sense whether we like them. How can these first impressions so often be accurate?

In this section of his book he describes the way a top tennis coach appears to know whether a shot is successful within a millisecond of seeing the racket hit the ball.

Not long ago, one of the world's top tennis coaches, a man named Vic Braden, began to notice something strange whenever he watched a tennis match. In tennis, players are given two chances to successfully hit a serve, and if they miss on their second chance, they are said to double-fault, and what Braden realized was that he always knew when a player was about to double-fault. A player would toss the ball up in the air and draw his racket back, and just as he was about to make contact, Braden would blurt out, 'Oh, no, double fault,' and sure enough, the ball would go wide or long or it would hit the net. It didn't seem to matter who was playing, man or woman, whether he was watching the match live or on television, or how well he knew the person serving. 'I was calling double faults on girls from Russia I'd never seen before in my life,' Braden says. Nor was Braden simply lucky. Lucky is when you call a coin toss correctly. But double-faulting is rare. In an entire match, a professional tennis player might hit hundreds of serves and double-fault no more than three or four times. One year, at the big professional tennis tournament at Indian Wells, near Braden's house in Southern California, he decided to keep track and found he correctly predicted sixteen out of seventeen double faults in the matches he watched. 'For a while it got so bad that I got scared,' Braden says. 'It literally scared me. I was getting twenty out of twenty right, and we're talking about guys who almost never double-fault.'

Braden is now in his seventies. When he was young, he was a world-class tennis player, and over the past fifty years, he has coached and counseled and known many of the greatest tennis players in the history of the game. He is a small and irrepressible man with the energy of someone half his age, and if you were to talk to people in the tennis world, they'd tell you that Vic Braden knows as much about the nuances and subtleties[1] of the game as any man alive. It isn't surprising, then, that Vic Braden should be really good at reading a serve in the blink of an eye. It really isn't any different from the ability of an art expert to look at the Getty kouros[2] and know, instantly, that it's a fake. Something in the way the tennis players hold themselves, or the way they toss the ball, or the fluidity of their motion, triggers something in his unconscious. He instinctively picks up the 'giss' of a double fault. He thin-slices some part of the service motion and – *blink!* – he just *knows*. But here's the catch: much to Braden's frustration, he simply cannot figure out *how* he knows.

'What did I see?' he says. 'I would lie in bed, thinking, How did I do this? I don't know. It drove me crazy. It tortured me. I'd go back and I'd go over the serve in my mind and I'd try to figure it out. Did they stumble? Did they take another step? Did they add a bounce to the ball – something that changed their motor program?' The evidence he used to draw his conclusions seemed to be buried somewhere in his unconscious, and he could not dredge it up.

This is the second critical fact about the thoughts and decisions that bubble up from our unconscious. Snap judgments are, first of all, enormously quick: they rely on the thinnest slices of experience. But they are also unconscious.

---

[1]**nuances and subtleties**   the tiny details that can make a difference
[2]**kouros**   Greek statue of a standing nude youth

Further reading

Malcolm Gladwell's journalism is entertaining as well as informative. His two best-known books, *Blink: The Power of Thinking without Thinking* (Penguin Books Ltd, 2006) and *The Tipping Point: How Little Things Can Make a Difference* (Abacus, 2002), are written in a straightforward way and help us to see the world more clearly. If you like writing that blends scientific and personal styles, you could also try Bill Bryson's *A Short History of Nearly Everything* (Black Swan, 2004).

The Selfish Giant

by Oscar Wilde

Oscar Wilde was a playwright and novelist who wrote during the late 19th and early 20th centuries. He was best known for his witty adult comedies but he also wrote some memorable children's stories. *The Selfish Giant* is a moral fable – a simple story with a powerful message about who we are and our responsibilities to others.

Every afternoon, as they were coming from school, the children used to go and play in the Giant's garden.

It was a large lovely garden, with soft green grass. Here and there over the grass stood beautiful flowers like stars, and there were twelve peach-trees that in the spring-time broke out into delicate blossoms of pink and pearl, and in the autumn bore rich fruit. The birds sat on the trees and sang so sweetly that the children used to stop their games in order to listen to them. 'How happy we are here!' they cried to each other.

One day the Giant came back. He had been to visit his friend the Cornish ogre, and had stayed with him for seven years. After the seven years were over he had said all that he had to say, for his conversation was limited, and he determined to return to his own castle. When he arrived he saw the children playing in the garden.

'What are you doing there?' he cried in a very gruff voice, and the children ran away.

'My own garden is my own garden,' said the Giant; 'anyone can understand that, and I will allow nobody to play in it but myself.' So he built a high wall all round it, and put up a notice-board.

TRESPASSERS
WILL BE
PROSECUTED

He was a very selfish Giant.

The poor children had now nowhere to play. They tried to play on the road, but the road was very dusty and full of hard stones, and they did not like it. They used to wander round the high wall when their lessons were over, and talk about the beautiful garden inside. 'How happy we were there,' they said to each other.

Then the Spring came, and all over the country there were little blossoms and little birds. Only in the garden of the Selfish Giant it was still winter. The birds did not care to sing in it as there were no children, and the trees forgot to blossom. Once a beautiful flower put its head out from the grass, but when it saw the notice-board it was so sorry for the children that it slipped back into the ground again, and went off to sleep. The only people who were pleased were the Snow and the Frost. 'Spring has forgotten this garden,' they cried, 'so we will live here all the year round.' The Snow covered up the grass with her great white cloak, and the Frost painted all the trees silver. Then they invited the North Wind to stay with them, and he came. He was wrapped in furs, and he roared all day about the garden, and blew the chimney-pots down. 'This is a delightful spot,' he said; 'we must ask the Hail on a visit.' So the Hail came. Every day for three hours he rattled on the roof of the castle till he broke most of the slates, and then he ran round and round the garden as fast as he could go. He was dressed in grey, and his breath was like ice.

'I cannot understand why the Spring is so late in coming,' said the Selfish Giant, as he sat at the window and looked out at his cold white garden; 'I hope there will be a change in the weather.'

But the Spring never came, nor the Summer. The Autumn gave golden fruit to every garden, but to the Giant's garden she gave none. 'He is too selfish,' she said. So it was always Winter there, and the North Wind, and the Hail, and the Frost, and the Snow danced about through the trees.

One morning the Giant was lying awake in bed when he heard some lovely music. It sounded so sweet to his ears that he thought it must be the King's musicians passing by. It was really only a little linnet[1] singing outside his window, but it was so long since he had heard a bird sing in his garden that it seemed to him to be the most beautiful music in the world. Then the Hail stopped dancing over his head, and the North Wind ceased roaring, and a delicious perfume came to him through the open casement. 'I believe the Spring has come at last,' said the Giant; and he jumped out of bed and looked out.

What did he see?

He saw a most wonderful sight. Through a little hole in the wall the children had crept in, and they were sitting in the branches of the trees. In every tree that he could see there was a little child. And the trees were so glad to have the children back again that they had covered themselves with blossoms, and were waving their arms gently above the children's heads. The birds were flying about and twittering with delight, and the flowers were looking up through the green grass and laughing. It was a lovely scene, only in one corner it was still winter. It was the farthest corner of the garden, and in it was standing a little boy. He was so small that he could not reach up to the branches of the tree, and he was wandering all round it, crying bitterly. The poor tree was still quite covered with frost and snow, and the North Wind was blowing and roaring above it. 'Climb up! little boy,' said the Tree, and it bent its branches down as low as it could; but the boy was too tiny.

And the Giant's heart melted as he looked out. 'How selfish I have been!' he said; 'now I know why the Spring would not come here. I will put that poor little boy on the top of the tree, and then I will knock down the wall, and my garden shall be the children's playground for ever and ever.' He was really very sorry for what he had done.

So he crept downstairs and opened the front door quite softly, and went out into the garden. But when the children saw him they were so frightened that they all ran away, and the garden became winter again. Only the little boy did not run, for his

---

[1]**linnet**   a small bird

eyes were so full of tears that he did not see the Giant coming.
And the Giant stole up behind him and took him gently in his
hand, and put him up into the tree. And the tree broke at once
into blossom, and the birds came and sang on it, and the little
boy stretched out his two arms and flung them round the
Giant's neck, and kissed him. And the other children, when they
saw that the Giant was not wicked any longer, came running
back, and with them came the Spring. 'It is your garden now, little children,' said the Giant, and he took a great axe and knocked
down the wall. And when the people were going to market at
twelve o'clock they found the Giant playing with the children in
the most beautiful garden they had ever seen.

All day long they played, and in the evening they came to
the Giant to bid him good-bye.

'But where is your little companion?' he said: 'the boy I put
into the tree.' The Giant loved him the best because he had
kissed him.

'We don't know,' answered the children; 'he has gone away.'

'You must tell him to be sure and come here to-morrow,' said
the Giant. But the children said that they did not know where he
lived, and had never seen him before; and the Giant felt very sad.

Every afternoon, when school was over, the children came and played with the Giant. But the little boy whom the Giant loved was never seen again. The Giant was very kind to all the children, yet he longed for his first little friend, and often spoke of him. 'How I would like to see him!' he used to say.

Years went over, and the Giant grew very old and feeble. He could not play about any more, so he sat in a huge armchair, and watched the children at their games, and admired his garden. 'I have many beautiful flowers,' he said; 'but the children are the most beautiful flowers of all.'

One winter morning he looked out of his window as he was dressing. He did not hate the Winter now, for he knew that it was merely the Spring asleep, and that the flowers were resting.

Suddenly he rubbed his eyes in wonder, and looked and looked. It certainly was a marvellous sight. In the farthest corner of the garden was a tree quite covered with lovely white blossoms. Its branches were all golden, and silver fruit hung down from them, and underneath it stood the little boy he had loved.

Downstairs ran the Giant in great joy, and out into the garden. He hastened across the grass, and came near to the child. And when he came quite close his face grew red with anger, and he said, 'Who hath dared to wound thee?' For on the palms of the child's hands were the prints of two nails, and the prints of two nails were on the little feet.

'Who hath dared to wound thee?' cried the Giant; 'tell me, that I may take my big sword and slay him.'

'Nay!' answered the child; 'but these are the wounds of Love.'

'Who art thou?' said the Giant, and a strange awe fell on him, and he knelt before the little child.

And the child smiled on the Giant, and said to him, 'You let me play once in your garden; today you shall come with me to my garden, which is Paradise.'

And when the children ran in that afternoon, they found the Giant lying dead under the tree, all covered with white blossoms.

Further reading

Oscar Wilde wrote a number of short stories, some specifically for children which are collected in *Oscar Wilde: Stories for Children* (Hodder Children's Books, 2006). You might also be interested in his dark and disturbing tale of a young man tempted by life's attractions – *The Picture of Dorian Gray* (Penguin Books Ltd, 2007).

An African Elegy

by Ben Okri

To an English Friend in Africa

For Daisy Waugh

Ben Okri is a Nigerian novelist and poet who now lives in London. He is known for his powerful use of language. In this poem, written for the writer Daisy Waugh, he gives advice to someone ten years or so younger than himself.

Be grateful for the freedom
To see other dreams.
Bless your loneliness as much as you drank
Of your former companionships.
All that you are experiencing now
Will become moods of future joys
So bless it all.

Do not think your way superior
To another's
Do not venture to judge
But see things with fresh and open eyes
Do not condemn[1]
But praise when you can
And when you can't, be silent.

Time now is a gift for you
A gift of freedom
To think and remember and understand
The ever perplexing past
And to re-create yourself anew
In order to transform time.

Live while you are alive.
Learn the ways of silence and wisdom
Learn to act, learn a new speech
Learn to be what you are in the seed of your spirit
Learn to free yourself from all the things
That have moulded you
And which limit your secret and undiscovered road.

Remember that all things which happen
To you are raw materials
Endlessly fertile
Endlessly yielding[2] of thoughts that could change
Your life and go on doing so forever.

Never forget to pray and be thankful
For all things good or bad on the rich road;
For everything is changeable
So long as you live while you are alive.

---

[1]**condemn**   criticise
[2]**yielding**   giving

Fear not, but be full of light and love;
Fear not, but be alert and receptive;[3]
Fear not, but act decisively when you should;
Fear not, but know when to stop;
Fear not, for you are loved by me;
Fear not, for death is not the real terror,
But life – magically – is.

Be joyful in your silence
Be strong in your patience
Do not try to wrestle with the universe
But be sometimes like water or air
Sometimes like fire
And constant like the earth.

Live slowly, think slowly, for time is a mystery.
Never forget that love
Requires always that you be
The greatest person you are capable of being,
Self-regenerating[4] and strong and gentle –
Your own hero and star.

Love demands the best in us
To always and in time overcome the worst
And lowest in our souls.
Love the world wisely.
It is love alone that is the greatest weapon
And the deepest and hardest secret.

So fear not, my friend.
The darkness is gentler than you think.

---

[3]**receptive**   open to experiences
[4]**self-regenerating**   able to become someone new

Be grateful for the manifold
Dreams of creation
And the many ways of the unnumbered peoples.

Be grateful for life as you live it.
And may a wonderful light
Always guide you on the unfolding road.

Further reading

As well as his poems, collected in *An African Elegy* (Vintage, 1997), you might enjoy Ben Okri's powerful descriptive fiction. His most famous novel is *The Famished Road* (Vintage, 1992).

I Found Love at the Supermarket Checkout

by Tom Hill

| Tom Hill reminds us that life can often surprise us. His life is suddenly transformed by a visit to the supermarket.

Friday evening, January 4, 2002. I'd just received a text message telling me I'd been stood up by someone I had yet to meet in person – we had arranged the date via the chatroom of a singles website. So instead of being in my bachelor pad, preparing for a romantic evening out, I found myself in Tesco, holding one of those bachelor baskets: two bottles of beaujolais,[1] a bag of rocket salad and a frozen pizza.

At the checkout, her eyes briefly met mine and we raised barely perceptible smiles for each other. She looked as if she'd been at that conveyor belt for the past seven hours. I'd been in suicidally tedious marketing meetings all day.

'Do you need any help with your packing?' she said in that singsong, 'don't-care-if-you-do-or-not' way.

'Do I really look like such a useless single bloke that I couldn't pack a carrier with half a dozen groceries?'

She looked up. 'Single? You? How come?'

I blushed, visibly. 'Well, I dunno . . . Married for 12 years, then she buggered off with a bloke half her age. What can you do?'

'She must've been mad. Seventeen pounds 60, please. Have you got a Clubcard?'

'Oh, Club . . . no . . . ' I stammered. I tried to say something clever. Anything, in fact, but nothing came out except, 'Thanks, see you later.'

It was as if an invisible rope was drawing me inexorably[2] towards the exit while my mind scrambled for something to say

---

[1]**beaujolais**   red wine from southern France
[2]**inexorably**   uncontrollably

before it was too late. The rope won. Thirty seconds later I was in the car park, trying to remember where I'd left my nondescript, middle-management Toyota saloon. Suddenly, it was as if something inside me upbraided[3] my timid ego. I threw the bag into the boot and, seizing the moment, re-entered the store and approached the customer services desk. I scribbled 'Call me' on the back of my business card and, after pausing a moment, added a potentially risqué solitary 'X'. I asked the supervisor to hand it to the woman on till 14 after I'd left the building. I remember thinking this simple impulsive act could change my life irrevocably.[4]

We met up in a quiet local pub the next evening. She was divorced, I was separated. I'd been trapped in a childless, faded marriage and an office job I hated. She'd been hemmed into her council estate by bringing up two kids while her husband worked away. Now they'd grown up and were soon to leave home. We went on more dates. After a couple of weeks, I said that if anything happened between us, it probably would never last – as soon as my decree absolute came through, I wanted to travel, to keep moving, to work my way around the world. I didn't feel that I was too far past it at 39. She was 41.

'Want a travelling companion?' she asked, in a matter-of-fact way.

Twelve months later we'd packed in our jobs. Her kids moved into a rented place together. We bought a nearly derelict two-up-two-down from our savings, in the dreariest part of the East Midlands. I'd hardly done more than put up a shelf in the past but, with patience, the place was fully renovated within a year. We lived in it briefly, finding work from agencies. Soon, after Linda had a cancer scare, we weighed the value of our time left on this earth versus the criminal squander of amassing[5] possessions. It wasn't a difficult decision. As soon as

---

[3]**upbraided**   criticised
[4]**irrevocably**   for ever and irreversibly
[5]**amassing**   getting, collecting

the all-clear arrived from the hospital, we remortgaged the place as a buy-to-let. We bought a long caravan and a big old Peugeot.

Last year we rode a Harley-Davidson from New York to San Francisco, then drove a camper van from Brisbane to Perth, house-sitting as we went. Now we make a living as we travel. Sometimes I pick up design work, or bear the pain of early starts as a middle-distance lorry driver. Lin will take anything from cleaning to catering. We have our own limited company and we pay our taxes like good citizens. We spend the winters doing odd jobs in the nicer parts of Europe.

We returned from Bergerac[6] this spring, having looked after two cats and a winery. Each morning, our breath hung in white clouds as we chainsawed dead trees for the wood burner. We walked for miles around the estate, casting long shadows in the stark winter sunlight. We shall be working in Cornwall until August, then a house-sit in a Kent village. From autumn, who knows? There is one certainty, though – wherever we travel, we will travel together.

---

[6]**Bergerac**   a market town in France

Further reading

As with the earlier piece by Barbara Brown, if you like this kind of real-life experience, look out for the weekly feature in *Weekend* magazine in Saturday's *Guardian*. If you're in the mood for some historical romance, try Daphne du Maurier's *Frenchman's Creek* (Virago Press Ltd, 2003) about an 18th-century aristocrat with a young family who falls for a handsome French pirate.

Warning to Children

by Robert Graves

Robert Graves is a poet, novelist and critic best known for his memoir of World War I, *Goodbye to All That*. In this poem, he aims to give advice to children. When we are young, adults often wish to give us advice, and sometimes it can leave us feeling frustrated and patronised. On other occasions we are grateful for the benefit of older people's thoughts and experiences. See what you think of the poet's warning.

Children, if you dare to think
Of the greatness, rareness, muchness,
Fewness of this precious only
Endless world in which you say
You live, you think of things like this:
Blocks of slate enclosing dappled
Red and green, enclosing tawny[1]
Yellow nets, enclosing white
And black acres of dominoes,
Where a neat brown paper parcel
Tempts you to untie the string.
In the parcel a small island,
On the island a large tree,
On the tree a husky[2] fruit.
Strip the husk and pare the rind off:
In the kernel[3] you will see
Blocks of slate enclosed by dappled
Red and green, enclosed by tawny
Yellow nets, enclosed by white
And black acres of dominoes,
Where the same brown paper parcel –

---

[1] **tawny**　an orange-brown colour
[2] **husky**　surrounded by a husk or rough shell
[3] **kernel**　the seed or stone in a fruit

Children, leave the string untied!
For who dares undo the parcel
Finds himself at once inside it,
On the island, in the fruit,
Blocks of slate about his head,
Finds himself enclosed by dappled
Green and red, enclosed by yellow
Tawny nets, enclosed by black
And white acres of dominoes,
With the same brown paper parcel
Still untied upon his knee.
And, if he then should dare to think
Of the fewness, muchness, rareness,
Greatness of this endless only
Precious world in which he says
He lives – he then unties the string.

Further reading

There are several good collections of poetry for children. One of the best is Brian Patten's *The Puffin Book of Utterly Brilliant Poetry* (Puffin Books, 1999). For a dark tale of a monstrous child, read Doris Lessing's *The Fifth Child* (Flamingo, 1998).

Activities

My Best Teacher

Before you read

1   Who is the teacher who has most influenced you? Think of someone from your primary or early secondary school. Write a short description of him or her. Make sure you answer all of these questions:
   - What was your teacher's name?
   - What was the name of the school you were at?
   - What subject(s) did your teacher teach?
   - What did he or she look like?
   - Why do you remember this teacher particularly well?
   - Is there one lesson or incident that sticks particularly in your mind?

What's it about?

2   Read the article and draw a quick sketch of Mr Hodgson. Label it using only the information given in the article.

3   Vic Reeves also describes the school he attended. Working in a small group, use a spider diagram to summarise what you learn about the school.

Thinking about the text

4   Read the final paragraph of the article again. How does the writer convey the sense of shock Vic Reeves and his schoolmates felt at the death of Mr Hodgson? Think about:
   - the tone of the writing
   - the length and structure of the sentences
   - the words used.

   Discuss your ideas with the rest of your class.

5   This text is based on an interview with Vic Reeves by journalist Marged Richards. It reads like personal writing ('When I think of him . . . '), but was actually written by Richards. Try a similar approach: interview a friend or member of your family about a teacher they particularly remember; then write a short article, using the first person ('I'), about their memories. Ask the person you interviewed to give you feedback on your article. Did you capture their memories accurately?

The Secret Life of Snap Decisions

Before you read

1   Are our first impressions of people usually accurate? Think back to the first time you met a certain person – did you judge them correctly? What has the biggest influence on your judgement (think about aspects of appearance, body language and speech)? Discuss your ideas with a partner and see whether you agree.

What's it about?

Read the extract and answer questions 2 to 4 by yourself. Then compare your answers with a partner's.

2   Who is Vic Braden? Where does he live? How old he is? What is his character?

3   Describe what you understand by 'double fault'.

4   Why did Vic Braden feel 'scared' when he watched the Indian Wells tournament?

Thinking about the text

5   How can you tell that this is a factual text, not fiction? What clues are there in the writing? How might it have been written differently if it was a made-up story? Discuss your ideas in a small group.

6   Students sometimes say that they can tell what a new teacher is like within minutes of his or her entering the room. *The Secret Life of Snap Decisions* suggests that they are right. Imagine you are writing guidelines for a teacher training college. What would you say are the five essential ingredients that make a good teacher? Write a set of five hints for new teachers. Underneath each hint, write a paragraph explaining it.

The Selfish Giant

Before you read

1   What are the ingredients of a good children's story? Use a spider diagram to record the key features you would expect to find in such a story. Discuss your ideas with the rest of your class.

What's it about?

Read the story and answer questions 2 to 4 by yourself. Then discuss your answers in a small group.

2   Look more closely at the setting for the story – the house, the garden, the wall and the tree. Draw a quick sketch, labelling the main features mentioned in the story.

3   Make a table with two columns headed 'The Selfish Giant' and 'The Little boy'. Complete the table with details about the two characters – such as what they look like, how they behave, how they treat others and how they change during the story.

4   This story was written more than a hundred years ago. What clues can you find in the text that tell you that it is not modern? Make a list of:

● words that we might not use today
● phrases and sentences that are expressed differently from how we might express them today.

Choose one phrase or sentence and write down how Oscar Wilde might have written it had he been writing the story today.

Thinking about the text

5   Some people love the ending of the story, finding it powerful and emotional. Other people strongly dislike it and feel embarrassed by it. Write a paragraph or two describing your response: what you like and dislike about the way the story ends.

6   Imagine you are one of the children who regularly tried to play in the Giant's garden. You knew him as a terrible, mean ogre. Suddenly he is transformed. Write a diary account which describes your surprise at the change in him. You could start like this: **I never thought I'd see what I saw today.**

An African Elegy

Before you read

1   If you were to give three pieces of advice to help a child do well in his or her first 14 or so years of life, what would they be? Discuss your ideas with the rest of your class.

What's it about?

2   Read the poem in its entirety, then look again at each section in turn. Write a sentence for each section, summarising what you think it is saying.

3   Ben Okri's writing often makes us think hard. Get into small groups and allocate each group a different line or phrase that is difficult to understand. In your group, build a spider diagram using any thoughts and ideas that the author's words bring to mind. When you think you know what your line or phrase means, present your findings to the rest of your class.

Thinking about the text

4   How can you tell that this is a poem? What if it were written out in a different layout, like this:

Be grateful for the freedom to see other dreams. Bless your loneliness as much as you drank of your former companionships . . .

Does it still feel like a poem even though it is set out like an article or story? Make a list of the features you notice in the language that tell you it is a poem. You might look at:
- the author's choice of words
- the use of rhythm
- any repetition of sounds.

Discuss your ideas with the rest of your class.

5   What do you like and dislike about the poem? Think about the way it is written as well as what it is about. Write two paragraphs giving your response.

I Found Love at the Supermarket Checkout

Before you read

1   Although we often try to plan our lives, events can take us by surprise. Take a minute or two to think about the biggest shock or surprise that has happened in your own life (either positive or negative) and talk to a partner about it.

2   Look at the title of this article. What do you predict will happen in it? Summarise your prediction in a sentence.

What's it about?

Read the article and answer questions 3 to 5 by yourself. Then compare your answers with a partner's.

3   **a**   What do we learn from the text about Tom Hill's life before he met Linda? Look for details about his lifestyle, his career and his family background.
   b   What do we learn about his new partner, Linda?
   c   Write down three things that the couple have in common.

4   Imagine the conversation between Tom and Linda when they decide to go travelling together. How might the subject have come up? How have their lives been transformed since they first met in the supermarket? Devise a role play to show what the conversation might have been like.

Thinking about the text

5   Make some notes on Tom and Linda's lives before and after they go travelling. Does the article make the lifestyle of travelling, doing various jobs along the way, sound attractive? Is it something you would like to do? Write a paragraph or two explaining your answer.

6   Look at the language of the text. Write down an example of:
   a   a statement   **e**   some formal language
   b   a question   **f**   some informal language
   c   some dialogue   **g**   a very long sentence
   d   a connective   **h**   a very short sentence.

Then write a paragraph summarising what you notice about the writer's use of language.

Warning to Children

Before you read

1   What does the word 'poem' make you think of? Use a spider dia-
    gram to make a note of the features you expect a poem to have.

What's it about?

2   Read the poem, then look at these statements. Find an example in
    the poem that supports or disproves each one.
    a   The poem is a warning about thinking too deeply about life.
    b   The poem is a warning not to accept things as they appear.
    c   The poem encourages us to see the beauty of nature under-
        neath things made by humans.
    d   The poem tells us to think for ourselves.
    e   The poem tells us that the world is a dangerous place.

    Discuss your ideas with the rest of your class.

3   What do you think is inside the paper parcel – is it a good or bad
    thing? Write a sentence explaining your answer.

Thinking about the text

4   Write a paragraph describing what you notice about the language
    of the poem. Use these questions to help you:
    a   How many sentences are there?
    b   How does the poet create a feeling of rhythm?
    c   Which words and sections are repeated? What is the effect of
        this repetition?
    d   Are there any rhymes?
    e   Is there alliteration (repetition of initial sounds, as in 'really
        rapid')? What effect does it have?

5   Working in a small group, put together a dramatic reading of the
    poem. Think about reading some parts as a group, some parts
    solo, some loud, some soft, some fast and some slow. Make it as
    dramatic as you can.

Compare and contrast

1   Look down the contents list for this section. Choose the text you most enjoyed reading, and the one you liked least. Write a paragraph or two explaining your choices.

2   Robert Graves's *Warning to Children* and Ben Okri's *An African Elegy* both give advice. Use these questions to help you compare the two poems.
    a   Write down one piece of specific advice from each poem.
    b   Write a sentence about each poem, summing up what advice you think the author is giving in general.
    c   Which poem is more optimistic (positive)?
    d   Which text is more difficult to understand?
    e   Write a sentence explaining any difference in the language of the two poems.

    Write a paragraph or two explaining which text you prefer, and why.

3   The texts in this section are all quite different. Create a diagram which shows what any of them have in common and how any of them are different in style or content.

4   Choose a character from three of the texts in this section and create a poster to show their main characteristics. Use these points to help you:
    ● Think about what each character is like at the beginning of the text and how they change.
    ● Draw an object that sums up each character.
    ● Find a quotation or comment that sums up each character.
    ● Think of a way to show visually the similarities and differences between the characters.

5   This section contains various different forms of texts. Think about which form suits which topic and finish these sentences:
    ● Poetry is best suited to . . .
    ● Non-fiction is best suited to . . .
    ● Fiction is best suited to . . .
    ● Overall the text I most enjoyed was . . . because . . .

3 Facing the world

The texts in this section take on a darker tone. Life suddenly seems tougher for many of the people at the heart of them. We start with Rudyard Kipling's poem of advice, *If*, and then there is a mixture of fiction and non-fiction texts which explore how people cope with personal challenges (Jerry in the story *Through the Tunnel*), potential and real disasters (Richard Branson and Ken Dornstein) and personal pain (Andrea Ashworth and Samantha Studley).

These texts all show us people taking on the world and facing up to real challenges. In the process they also show us the power of the human spirit.

Activities

1   This section is all about challenges. Undertake a survey within your family or class, asking people what is the biggest challenge they have faced in their life. Present your findings as a poster.

2   What are the most important qualities you think people need to develop in order to cope with life's challenges? Look at the list below and, with a partner, discuss what you think each word means. Then decide which you think are the *three* most important qualities you would look for in someone.

leadership	*trustworthiness*	*integrity*	*courage*
honesty	*optimism*	*perseverance*	*resilience*

3   People sometimes say that young people lack role models – people that they can look up to and admire. Do you agree? Who do you consider to be your role models? Think of someone from your personal life (family, teacher, friend) and someone in the public eye (actor, politician, sports player). Write a short paragraph about each person, describing the qualities that make him or her a role model for you.

If

by Rudyard Kipling

Rudyard Kipling was a novelist and poet at the start of the 20th century. You might know him best for his *Jungle Book* stories. His poem, *If,* is a famous poem which gives advice on how to survive in life.

If you can keep your head when all about you
    Are losing theirs and blaming it on you,
If you can trust yourself when all men doubt you,
    But make allowance for their doubting too;
If you can wait and not be tired by waiting,
    Or being lied about, don't deal in lies,
Or being hated, don't give way to hating,
    And yet don't look too good, nor talk too wise:

If you can dream – and not make dreams your master;
    If you can think – and not make thoughts your aim;
If you can meet with Triumph and Disaster
    And treat those two imposters[1] just the same;
If you can bear to hear the truth you've spoken
    Twisted by knaves to make a trap for fools,
Or watch the things you gave your life to, broken,
    And stoop and build 'em up with worn-out tools:

If you can make one heap of all your winnings
    And risk it on one turn of pitch-and-toss,[2]
And lose, and start again at your beginnings
    And never breathe a word about your loss;
If you can force your heart and nerve and sinew
    To serve your turn long after they are gone,
And so hold on when there is nothing in you
    Except the Will which says to them: 'Hold on!'

If you can talk with crowds and keep your virtue,[3]
    Or walk with Kings – nor lose the common touch,
If neither foes nor loving friends can hurt you,
    If all men count with you, but none too much;
If you can fill the unforgiving minute
    With sixty seconds' worth of distance run,
Yours is the Earth and everything that's in it,
    And – which is more – you'll be a Man, my son!

Further reading

You can read Rudyard Kipling's poems in *Rudyard Kipling: The Complete Verse* (Kyle Cathie, 2006). You might also find it interesting to read *The Jungle Book* (Penguin Books Ltd, 1996) and compare it with the two Disney movie versions (animation and live action).

---

[1]**imposters**   people who pretend to be someone else
[2]**pitch-and-toss**   traditional game
[3]**virtue**   goodness

Through the Tunnel

by Doris Lessing

> Born in Persia (now known as Iran), Doris Lessing is a very well-respected British writer famous for her novels and short stories. She also writes science fiction. This story describes a young boy who decides to push himself to the limits of his own endurance by holding his breath and swimming underwater, 'through the tunnel'.

Going to the shore on the first morning of the holiday, the young English boy stopped at a turning of the path and looked down at a wild and rocky bay, and then over to the crowded beach he knew so well from other years. His mother walked on in front of him, carrying a bright striped bag in one hand. Her other arm, swinging loose, was very white in the sun. The boy watched that white, naked arm, and turned his eyes, which had a frown behind them, towards the bay and back again to his mother. When she felt he was not with her, she swung around. 'Oh, there you are, Jerry!' she said. She looked impatient, then smiled. 'Why, darling, would you rather not come with me? Would you rather – ' She frowned, conscientiously worrying over what amusements he might secretly be longing for, which she had been too busy or too careless to imagine. He was very familiar with that anxious, apologetic smile. Contrition[1] sent him running after her. And yet, as he ran, he looked back over his shoulder at the wild bay; and all morning, as he played on the safe beach, he was thinking of it.

Next morning, when it was time for the routine of swimming and sunbathing, his mother said, 'Are you tired of the usual beach, Jerry? Would you like to go somewhere else?'

'Oh, no!' he said quickly, smiling at her out of that unfailing impulse of contrition – a sort of chivalry.[2] Yet, walking

---

[1]**contrition**   guilt
[2]**chivalry**   courteous behaviour towards women

down the path with her, he blurted out, 'I'd like to go and have a look at those rocks down there.'

She gave the idea her attention. It was a wild-looking place, and there was no one there; but she said, 'Of course, Jerry. When you've had enough, come to the big beach. Or just go straight back to the villa, if you like.' She walked away, that bare arm, now slightly reddened from yesterday's sun, swinging. And he almost ran after her again, feeling it unbearable that she should go by herself, but he did not.

She was thinking, Of course he's old enough to be safe without me. Have I been keeping him too close? He mustn't feel he ought to be with me. I must be careful.

He was an only child, eleven years old. She was a widow. She was determined to be neither possessive nor lacking in devotion. She went worrying off to her beach.

As for Jerry, once he saw that his mother had gained her beach, he began the steep descent to the bay. From where he was, high up among red-brown rocks, it was a scoop of moving bluish green fringed with white. As he went lower, he saw that it spread among small promontories and inlets of rough, sharp rock, and the crisping, lapping surface showed stains of purple and darker blue. Finally, as he ran sliding and scraping down the last few yards, he saw an edge of white surf and the shallow, luminous movement of water over white sand, and, beyond that, a solid heavy blue.

He ran straight into the water and began swimming. He was a good swimmer. He went out fast over the gleaming sand, over a middle region where rocks lay like discoloured monsters under the surface and then he was in the real sea – a warm sea where irregular cold currents from the deep water shocked his limbs.

When he was so far out that he could look back not only on the little bay but past the promontory that was between it and the big beach, he floated on the buoyant surface and looked for his mother. There she was, a speck of yellow under an umbrella that looked like a slice of orange peel. He swam back to shore, relieved at being sure she was there, but all at once very lonely.

On the edge of a small cape that marked the side of the bay away from the promontory was a loose scatter of rocks. Above them, some boys were stripping off their clothes. They came running, naked, down to the rocks. The English boy swam towards them, but kept his distance at a stone's throw. They were of that coast; all of them were burned smooth dark brown and speaking a language he did not understand. To be with them, of them, was a craving that filled his whole body. He swam a little closer; they turned and watched him with narrowed, alert dark eyes. Then one smiled and waved. It was enough. In a minute, he had swum in and was on the rocks beside them, smiling with a desperate, nervous supplication.³ They shouted cheerful greetings at him; and then, as he preserved his nervous, uncomprehending smile, they understood that he was a foreigner strayed from his own beach, and they proceeded to forget him. But he was happy. He was with them.

They began diving again and again from a high point into a well of blue sea between rough, pointed rocks. After they had dived and come up, they swam around, hauled themselves up, and waited their turn to dive again. They were big boys – men, to Jerry. He dived, and they watched him; and when he swam around to take his place, they made way for him. He felt he was accepted and he dived again, carefully, proud of himself.

Soon the biggest of the boys poised himself, shot down into the water, and did not come up. The others stood about, watching. Jerry, after waiting for the sleek brown head to appear, let out a yell of warning; they looked at him idly and turned their eyes back towards the water. After a long time, the boy came up on the other side of a big dark rock, letting the air out of his lungs in a sputtering gasp and a shout of triumph. Immediately the rest of them dived in. One moment, the morning seemed full of chattering boys; the next, the air and the surface of the water were empty. But through the heavy blue, dark shapes could be seen moving and groping.

---

³**supplication**   trying hard to be liked

Jerry dived, shot past the school of underwater swimmers, saw a black wall of rock looming at him, touched it, and bobbed up at once to the surface, where the wall was a low barrier he could see across. There was no one visible; under him, in the water, the dim shapes of the swimmers had disappeared. Then one, and then another of the boys came up on the far side of the barrier of rock, and he understood that they had swum through some gap or hole in it. He plunged down again. He could see nothing through the stinging salt water but the blank rock. When he came up the boys were all on the diving rock, preparing to attempt the feat again. And now, in a panic of failure, he yelled up, in English, 'Look at me! Look!' and he began splashing and kicking in the water like a foolish dog.

They looked down gravely, frowning. He knew the frown. At moments of failure, when he clowned to claim his mother's attention, it was with just this grave, embarrassed inspection that she rewarded him. Through his hot shame, feeling the pleading grin on his face like a scar that he could never remove, he looked up at the group of big brown boys on the rock and shouted, *'Bonjour! Merci! Au revoir! Monsieur, monsieur!'* while he hooked his fingers round his ears and waggled them.

Water surged into his mouth; he choked, sank, came up. The rock, lately weighted with boys, seemed to rear up out of the water as their weight was removed. They were flying down past him now, into the water; the air was full of falling bodies. Then the rock was empty in the hot sunlight. He counted one, two, three . . .

At fifty, he was terrified. They must all be drowning beneath him, in the watery caves of the rock. At a hundred, he stared around him at the empty hillside, wondering if he should yell for help. He counted faster, faster, to hurry them up, to bring them to the surface quickly, to drown them quickly – anything rather than the terror of counting on and on into the blue emptiness of the morning. And then, at a hundred and sixty, the water beyond the rock was full of boys blowing like brown whales. They swam back to the shore without a look at him.

He climbed back to the diving rock and sat down, feeling the hot roughness of it under his thighs. The boys were gathering up their bits of clothing and running off along the shore to another promontory. They were leaving to get away from him. He cried openly, fists in his eyes. There was no one to see him, and he cried himself out.

It seemed to him that a long time had passed, and he swam out to where he could see his mother. Yes, she was still there, a yellow spot under an orange umbrella. He swam back to the big rock, climbed up, and dived into the blue pool among the fanged and angry boulders. Down he went, until he touched the wall of rock again. But the salt was so painful in his eyes that he could not see.

He came to the surface, swam to shore and went back to the villa to wait for his mother. Soon she walked slowly up the path, swinging her striped bag, the flushed, naked arm dangling beside her. 'I want some swimming goggles,' he panted, defiant and beseeching.

She gave him a patient, inquisitive look as she said casually, 'Well, of course, darling.'

But now, now, now! He must have them this minute, and no other time. He nagged and pestered until she went with him to a shop. As soon as she had bought the goggles, he grabbed them from her hand as if she were going to claim them for herself, and was off, running down the steep path to the bay.

Jerry swam out to the big barrier rock, adjusted the goggles, and dived. The impact of the water broke the rubber-enclosed vacuum, and the goggles came loose. He understood that he must swim down to the base of the rock from the surface of the water. He fixed the goggles tight and firm, filled his lungs, and floated, face down, on the water. Now, he could see. It was as if he had eyes of a different kind – fish eyes that showed everything clear and delicate and wavering in the bright water.

Under him, six or seven feet down, was a floor of perfectly clean, shining white sand, rippled firm and hard by the tides. Two greyish shapes steered there, like long, rounded pieces of wood or slate. They were fish. He saw them nose towards each other, poise motionless, make a dart forward, swerve off, and come around again. It was like a water dance. A few inches above them the water sparkled as if sequins were dropping through it. Fish again – myriads of minute fish, the length of his fingernail, were drifting through the water, and in a moment he could feel the innumerable tiny touches of them against his limbs. It was like swimming in flaked silver. The great rock the big boys had swum through rose sheer out of the white sand – black, tufted lightly with greenish weed. He could see no gap in it. He swam down to its base.

Again and again he rose, took a big chestful of air, and went down again. Again and again he groped over the surface of the rock, feeling it, almost hugging it in the desperate need to find the entrance. And then, once, while he was clinging to the black wall, his knees came up and he shot his feet out forward and they met no obstacle. He had found the hole.

He gained the surface, clambered about the stones that littered the barrier rock until he found a big one, and, with this in his arms, let himself down over the side of the rock. He dropped, with the weight, straight to the sandy floor. Clinging tight to the anchor of stone, he lay on his side and looked in under the dark shelf at the place where his feet had gone. He could see the hole. It was an irregular, dark gap but he could not see deep into it. He let go of his anchor, clung with his hands to the edges of the hole, and tried to push himself in.

He got his head in, found his shoulders jammed, moved them in sideways, and was inside as far as his waist. He could see nothing ahead. Something soft and clammy touched his mouth; he saw a dark frond moving against the greyish rock, and panic filled him. He thought of octopuses, of clinging weed. He pushed himself out backwards and caught a glimpse, as he retreated, of a harmless tentacle of seaweed drifting in the mouth of the tunnel. But it was enough. He reached the sunlight, swam to shore, and lay on the diving rock. He looked down into the blue well of water. He knew he must find his way through that cave, or hole, or tunnel, and out the other side.

First, he thought, he must learn to control his breathing. He let himself down into the water with another big stone in his arms, so that he could lie effortlessly on the bottom of the sea. He counted. One, two, three. He counted steadily. He could hear the movement of blood in his chest. Fifty-one, fifty-two . . . His chest was hurting. He let go of the rock and went up into the air. He saw the sun was low. He rushed to the villa and found his mother at her supper. She said only, 'Did you enjoy yourself?' and he said, 'Yes.'

All night the boy dreamed of the water-filled cave in the rock, and as soon as breakfast was over he went to the bay.

That night, his nose bled badly. For hours he had been underwater, learning to hold his breath, and now he felt weak and dizzy. His mother said, 'I shouldn't overdo things, darling, if I were you.'

That day and the next, Jerry exercised his lungs as if everything, the whole of his life, all that he would become, depended upon it. Again his nose bled at night, and his mother insisted on his coming with her the next day. It was a torment to him to waste a day of his careful self-training, but he stayed with her on that other beach, which now seemed a place for small children, a place where his mother might lie safe in the sun. It was not his beach.

He did not ask for permission, on the following day, to go to his beach. He went, before his mother could consider the complicated rights and wrongs of the matter. A day's rest, he discovered, had improved his count by ten. The big boys had made the passage while he counted a hundred and sixty. He had been counting fast, in his fright. Probably now, if he tried, he could get through that long tunnel, but he was not going to try yet. A curious, most unchildlike persistence, a controlled impatience, made him wait. In the meantime, he lay underwater on the white sand, littered now by stones he had brought down from the upper air, and studied the entrance to the tunnel. He knew every jut and corner of it, as far as it was possible to see. It was as if he already felt its sharpness about his shoulders.

He sat by the clock in the villa, when his mother was not near, and checked his time. He was incredulous and then proud to find he could hold his breath without strain for two minutes. The words, 'two minutes,' authorised by the clock, brought close the adventure that was so necessary to him.

In another four days, his mother said casually one morning, they must go home. On the day before they left, he would do it. He would do it if it killed him, he said defiantly to himself. But two days before they were to leave – a day of triumph when he increased his count by fifteen – his nose bled so badly that he turned dizzy and had to lie limply over the big rock like a bit of seaweed, watching the thick red blood flow on to the rock and trickle slowly down to the sea. He was frightened. Supposing he turned dizzy in the tunnel? Supposing he died there, trapped? Supposing – his head went around, in the hot sun, and he almost gave up. He thought he would return to the house and lie down, and next summer, perhaps when he had another year's growth in him – *then* he would go through the hole.

But even after he had made the decision, or thought he had, he found himself sitting up on the rock and looking down into the water; and he knew that now, this moment, when his nose had only just stopped bleeding, when his head was still sore and throbbing – this was the moment when he would try. If he did not do it now, he never would. He was trembling with fear that he would not go; and he was trembling with horror at that long, long tunnel under the rock, under the sea. Even in the open sunlight, the barrier rock seemed very wide and very heavy; tons of rock pressed down on where he would go. If he died there, he would lie until one day – perhaps not before next year – those big boys would swim into it and find it blocked.

He put on his goggles, fitted them tight, tested the vacuum. His hands were shaking. Then he chose the biggest stone he could carry and slipped over the edge of the rock until half of him was in the cool, enclosing water and half in the hot sun. He looked up once at the empty sky, filled his lungs once, twice, and then sank fast to the bottom with the stone. He let it go and began to count. He took the edges of the hole in his hands and drew himself into it, wriggling his shoulders in sideways as he remembered he must, kicking himself along with his feet.

Soon he was clear inside. He was in a small rock-bound hole filled with yellowish-grey water. The water was pushing him up against the roof. The roof was sharp and pained his back. He pulled himself along with his hands – fast, fast – and used his legs as levers. His head knocked against something; a sharp pain dizzied him. Fifty, fifty-one, fifty-two . . . He was without light, and the water seemed to press upon him with the weight of rock. Seventy-one, seventy-two . . . There was no strain on his lungs. He felt like an inflated balloon, his lungs were so light and easy, but his head was pulsing.

He was being continually pressed against the sharp roof, which felt slimy as well as sharp. Again he thought of octopuses, and wondered if the tunnel might be filled with weed that could tangle him. He gave himself a panicky, convulsive kick forward, ducked his head, and swam. His feet and hands moved freely, as if in open water. The hole must have widened out. He thought he must be swimming fast, and he was frightened of banging his head if the tunnel narrowed.

A hundred, a hundred and one . . . The water paled. Victory filled him. His lungs were beginning to hurt. A few more strokes and he would be out. He was counting wildly; he said a hundred and fifteen, and then, a long time later, a hundred and fifteen again. The water was a clear jewel-green all around him. Then he saw, above his head, a crack running up through the rock. Sunlight was falling through it, showing the clean, dark rock of the tunnel, a single mussel shell, and darkness ahead.

He was at the end of what he could do. He looked up at the crack as if it were filled with air and not water, as if he could put his mouth to it and draw air. A hundred and fifteen, he heard himself say inside his head – but he had said that long ago. He must go on into the blackness ahead, or he would drown. His head was swelling, his lungs cracking. A hundred and fifteen, a hundred and fifteen pounded through his head, and he feebly clutched at rocks in the dark, pulling himself forward, leaving the brief space of sunlit water behind. He felt he was dying. He was no longer quite conscious. He struggled on in the darkness between lapses into unconsciousness. An immense, swelling pain filled his head, and then the darkness cracked with an explosion of green light. His hands, groping forward, met nothing; and his feet, kicking back, propelled him out into the open sea.

He drifted to the surface, his face turned up to the air. He was gasping like a fish. He felt he would sink now and drown; he could not swim the few feet back to the rock. Then he was clutching it and pulling himself up on to it. He lay face down, gasping. He could see nothing but a red-veined, clotted dark. His eyes must have burst, he thought; they were full of blood. He tore off his goggles and a gout of blood went into the sea. His nose was bleeding, and the blood had filled the goggles.

He scooped up handfuls of water from the cool, salty sea, to splash on his face, and did not know whether it was blood or salt water he tasted. After a time, his heart quietened, his eyes cleared, and he sat up. He could see the local boys diving and playing half a mile away. He did not want them. He wanted nothing but to get back home and lie down.

In a short while, Jerry swam to the shore and climbed slowly up the path to the villa. He flung himself on his bed and slept, waking at the sound of feet on the path outside. His mother was coming back. He rushed to the bathroom, thinking she must not see his face with bloodstains, or tearstains, on it. He came out of the bathroom and met her as she walked into the villa, smiling, her eyes lighting up.

'Have a nice morning?' she asked, laying her hand on his warm brown shoulder a moment.

'Oh yes, thank you,' he said.

'You look a bit pale.' And then, sharp and anxious, 'How did you bang your head?'

'Oh, just banged it,' he told her.

She looked at him closely. He was strained; his eyes were glazed-looking. She was worried. And then she said to herself, Oh, don't fuss! Nothing can happen. He can swim like a fish.

They sat down to lunch together.

'Mummy,' he said, 'I can stay under water for two minutes – three minutes, at least.' It came bursting out of him.

'Can you, darling?' she said. 'Well, I shouldn't overdo it. I don't think you ought to swim any more today.'

She was ready for a battle of wills, but he gave in at once. It was no longer of the least importance to go to the bay.

Further reading

Doris Lessing's short stories are a wonderful and powerful read. You will find more in *Collected Stories 1* and *Collected Stories 2* (Flamingo, 2003). To read a very different account of overcoming childhood traumas, see Maya Angelou's autobiography, *I Know Why the Caged Bird Sings* (New Windmill, Heinemann Educational Publishers, 1995).

Almost Drowning

by Richard Branson

Richard Branson is a famous businessman who is best known for his Virgin empire of shops, services and airline. Here he recalls a 'wonderful' holiday in Mexico which suddenly turns to near tragedy.

In the summer of 1974 we decided to go on holiday to get away from it all and try to patch up our marriage. Kristen chose Cozumel off the coast of Mexico on the grounds that the telephones wouldn't work there and nobody at Virgin would be able to get hold of me. We spent two wonderful weeks there and ended up on the Yucatán peninsula. I had never done any deep-sea fishing, and one night in the bar of a small port we started talking to some other tourists who told us that this was the best place in the world for marlin and sailfish. We agreed that we would ask a fisherman to take us out the next day.

Although the next day seemed bright and clear to us, the fishermen were wary about going out. In bad English and with the help of Kristen's broken Spanish, they explained that there was the possibility of a storm.

'Come on,' I pleaded. 'We've only got a couple more days here. We'll pay you double.'

They accepted the incentive,[1] and together with the two other tourists from the bar, who also paid the double fare, we set out. We started fishing and took turns at manning the rods. Soon Kristen caught a large sailfish, which jumped about eight feet out of the water and took almost forty minutes to wind in. We released it, and started fishing again. Both the other tourists caught marlin before one came for my bait. Marlin often knock the fish up out of the water with their spikes and then catch them in the air. We watched the fin come up behind my bait and then the bait spun up in the air

---

[1] **incentive**   encouragement of extra money

and the huge black and silver side of the marlin rose above the water to take it.

As I played the marlin, we suddenly noticed that it was growing dark and cold. Behind us the clouds were gathering and it soon became clear that we were going to be caught up in the predicted storm. Large drops of rain hit the deck. Without warning one of the fishermen pulled out his knife and cut my line. The abrupt loss of my fish and the thought of it swimming around trailing two hundred yards of nylon from its gullet sickened me. We had released the other fish we had caught, but this marlin was being consigned to certain death attached to the length of line.

The fishermen started up the engine to head home, but rather than heading back to the shore the boat started drifting around in circles. The rudder had jammed. The sea rose around us, and the waves started breaking over the stern. Kristen was shaking uncontrollably. We were soaked through, and freezing cold. The storm clouds completely blocked out the sun and it became dark, so dark that it might have been night. We went down into the tiny cabin, which was full of smoke from the engine. One of the tourists was sick. I opened the window, but the smell of vomit and diesel remained. The boat was being so badly smashed up that we were sure she would sink.

After an hour of the worst storm any of us had ever experienced, the wind and rain abruptly stopped. The sea was still running very high, with the waves towering over ten feet above us. It was eerily still. We must have been in the eye of the storm. For a while there was bright sunlight. Then we saw the other side of the storm coming, a solid black line above the horizon, growing more threatening as it came nearer.

'Richard, I think we should swim for it,' Kristen said. 'This boat won't take another storm.'

'You're mad,' the other tourists said. 'Stay on board.'

Kristen and I agreed that the boat wouldn't survive another pounding. We argued with the fishermen and the tourists, who disagreed. The shore was about two miles away.

The sea around us was an ugly, matt black colour, swelling high and boiling, with white foam flecked across the surface. I was terrified but I decided that Kristen was right. She had been a good long-distance swimmer at school, and she gave me the only pair of flippers on board. We stripped off to our underwear, and the fishermen gave us a plank of wood. We all wished each other the best of luck and then Kristen and I jumped overboard. Almost immediately the current swept us past the boat and up the coast. We lost sight of the boat and concentrated on kicking out for the coast, which we could see only from the tops of the waves. Kristen led the way and I tried to keep up with her. As well as fishing for marlin, we had also been on the lookout for sharks, and as we swam I started imagining that the first thing I would feel would be a vast fish rearing up beneath me, knocking me sideways just as the marlin had dealt with my bait, and ripping into my stomach and legs.

'Don't kick too hard,' Kristen shouted in my ear. 'You don't want to get cramp.'

We swam across the current, not worrying that we were being carried up the coast just as long as we weren't being taken out to sea. Slowly we came closer. We had been in the water for almost two hours before I knew that we would definitely make land. The coast was at first just a smudged green line, then we could see the trees, and finally a mud beach. Even after we could see the beach it took us another hour to get there. We hauled our way up through the surf and collapsed on to the sand. We had swum in the stormy sea for almost three hours. We were freezing cold, and our hands and feet were white and wrinkled. We clung on to each other, and told ourselves that after that we would always be together.

'We've got to get back down to the port,' she said. 'We've got to get a rescue party out to save the boat. They might have a lifeboat.'

We started running down the peninsula. We had to fight our way through some mangrove swamps and finally arrived in the tiny port after an hour, half-naked, trembling with shock and exhaustion, and with our feet bleeding.

At the port we found the captain of the local car ferry and Kristen explained to him that there was a boat out at sea in trouble with a jammed rudder. He agreed to go out to try to rescue the fishing boat. He lent us some clothes and at once we set out to sea. Within fifteen minutes the second storm hit. It was far worse than the first one and it picked up the car ferry, which was a big heavy boat, and tossed it around like flotsam. We couldn't believe that, after our first escape, we were back at sea in the storm. After ten minutes the captain told us that he was turning back. It was hopeless. Although we wanted to go on, we could see that the ferry was in danger of capsizing.

The fishing boat was never found. Kristen and I left Mexico two days later. I had to learn to live with the question of whether the fishermen would have gone out to sea that day if it hadn't been for us. Two fishermen and two tourists had drowned, and a fishing boat was lost. I wondered if we and the other two tourists should have waved a handful of dollars in front of them.

Further reading

Richard Branson's autobiography, *Losing My Virginity* (Virgin Books, 2005), gives a lively account of his unconventional schooldays and how he became Britain's most famous entrepreneur. For an account of a very different adventure at sea, read Peter Benchley's *Jaws* (Pan, 2004), one of the most famous thrillers of them all.

The Boy Who Fell out of the Sky

by Ken Dornstein

The next few texts show us how resilient human beings can be – how we can come to terms with events that push us to our emotional limits. In December 1988, Pan Am Flight 103 was brought down by a terrorist bomb. 270 passengers, crew and civilians on the ground in Lockerbie, Scotland, were killed, including the brother of American journalist Ken Dornstein. Here he recalls how he and his father reacted and then came to terms with the events.

The night my brother died, I slept fine, back in my old bed in the old house where I grew up. I came downstairs late the next morning. My father and stepmother had left for work, but I was on my first day home for Christmas break from college. I had nothing to do and the entire day to do it. I found the newspaper laid out on the kitchen table. The headline ran in giant letters across the front page – 'Plane with 259 aboard crashes, destroys 40 homes in Scotland.' I started to read.

'LOCKERBIE, Scotland – A Pan Am jumbo jet bound for New York with 259 people, many of them Christmas travellers, crashed last night into this Scottish village, exploding into a huge fireball and setting ablaze dozens of homes and cars. No survivors from the Boeing 747 were found . . . The cause of the crash was not immediately clear.' There were also pictures – a Scottish police officer peering into the plane's crushed cockpit in a field; houses and cars on fire; a woman collapsed on the floor of JFK Airport[1] (she'd just been told that her daughter was on the plane). I skimmed the stories. I checked the sports page and the police blotter in the suburban 'Neighbours' section. A pizza-delivery man had been robbed at knifepoint not too far from where I lived. News is just news to those not immediately

---

[1]**JFK Airport**   the main airport in New York, named after former US President John F. Kennedy

affected, and my brother was not supposed to fly until later in the week.

I have come to think of the impact of my brother's death in dramatic terms: a curtain dropping on my youth, a terrible storm that left me shipwrecked, the start of a new life. But this language came much later. Events unfolded in a more everyday way: the phone rang and my father, home early from work, answered it. A sales agent from the airline said she might have some unfortunate news about a David Dornstein. *Is this the family of David Dornstein?*

The agent said she needed to check the final passenger list. She said she needed to cross-reference one thing with another. She said she needed to speak to her supervisor. She said she needed to get people in London or Scotland or New York or somewhere to 'sign off'. She said things were still a little confused. So could you please bear with us? *Could you please hold?* My father waited on hold by himself initially, and then he called upstairs to me. I found him at his desk. 'Pan Am is on the phone,' he said. David boarded the plane at Heathrow, the woman from the airline had told him, but for some reason she wasn't ready to say that he was on the plane when it exploded. My father held the phone away from his ear and let his head slump. I could hear the airline's hold music through an amplifier my father had put on the phone because he has a bad ear: Dionne Warwick's *Do You Know the Way to San Jose*; a Muzak version of *When I'm Sixty-Four*. The phone call from Pan Am was strange, and the news likely tragic, but the experience of being on hold was familiar. It was as if we had called to book a flight, a winter getaway.

When the woman from Pan Am came back on the phone, my father mainly listened. What happened next for my father is not for me to tell. He may not even recall the details; we've never spoken about it. But I remember my own reaction, and it still troubles me. I didn't cry or put my head in my hands or collapse like the lady from the picture at JFK. I was still. I understood the loss as my father's, for the most part, and I thought about how to console him. I looked down from above as the scene played out: those two pitiable[2] souls, my father and me. I felt sorry for them, like I might feel for the survivors of an earthquake somewhere; sorry like I'd initially felt for the victims of Flight 103 when I read about them in the paper that morning – which is to say, not that sorry at all. It was intolerable for me to have a personal connection to this story, so I simply decided not to.

My father began making calls – one to a friend to cancel dinner plans, another to my sister, who said she'd be over right away. My stepmother walked in from work and collapsed in the doorway after hearing the news. My father helped her to a chair. I didn't know what to do. I walked back upstairs. The book I'd been reading was still propped open at the place I'd left off. A glazed chocolate doughnut sat half eaten on a white napkin. I am embarrassed to say that I finished it. I was hungry. Now what?

The cabin of a passenger jet is like a big balloon that is blown up and deflated every time a plane takes off and lands, sealing the passengers inside an environment that is safe and comfortable

---

[2]**pitiable**   making us feel a sense of pity or extreme sadness

while the plane cruises at 30,000ft. When the fuselage[3] is rup-
tured, the pressurisation balloon pops and the cabin begins to
rapidly decompress. Gases in the sinuses, ears, lungs, stomach,
and gastrointestinal system expand rapidly, to reach equilibrium
with the thinner outside air, swelling the abdomen and bulging
the eyes, forcing air out of the lungs. What does this feel like? One
woman who experienced a rapid decompression on a 747 a few
months after Lockerbie described the sudden drop in pressure as
'a knife through my head'. Another woman talked of a wind so
loud that she couldn't hear her husband next to her screaming.
The survivor of a different rapid decompression wrote a shaky-
handed note to his family on the back of the in-flight magazine:

Overhead blown out. Rows 1–9. Many missing pieces. Can see sky &
clouds . . . Fibreglass insulation throughout cabin. Terrible [illegible]
noise . . . No time left. Love, Dad.

The passengers aboard Flight 103, the *Clipper Maid of the Seas*,
did not have time to write notes, but did they know what was
happening to them? A jury in Brooklyn would take up this
question a few years later, after Pan Am was found guilty of wil-
ful misconduct in allowing the bomb on to Flight 103. The jury
was asked to determine whether any of the passengers qualified
for 'pre-death pain and suffering' – that is, compensation for
the horror of realising that they were about to die – with the
most money to be awarded to those who suffered this knowledge the longest.

Experts on both sides testified about 'useful conscious time',
'occupant kinematics',[4] 'human terminal velocities' and 'flail
phenomena' – the tendency of the human body to spread out like
a bird in freefall. Both sides agreed that passengers aboard Flight
103 faced extreme hazards – the cold, the wind, the altitude, people and objects loose in the cabin. The passengers' lawyer said
that none of these things alone meant instantaneous death, but

---

[3]**fuselage**   main body of an aircraft
[4]**kinematics**   branch of mechanics that deals with how objects move

Pan Am's lawyer claimed that the combination was unsurvivable. He told the jury: 'We don't know what happened to any individual person on that aeroplane. Isn't that really a blessing? Your verdict should send a comforting message to the families. It should tell them that there is no evidence that your loved one suffered in this accident. Give them that peace of mind.'

Pan Am got its verdict, but I wasn't much comforted. It took a few seconds after the bomb blast for the cockpit to 'unzipper' from the main cabin – wasn't this enough time for people on board to register that something had gone wrong? When the space shuttle *Challenger* suffered an explosive decompression at 48,000ft, pilot Michael J. Smith's last recorded words were 'Uh-oh'. If David or any of the others on Flight 103 had a last thought, I imagine it would have been something like that.

Years later I flew to the Netherlands to see a judge deliver the verdict in the trial of the two Libyans charged with the bombing of Flight 103 (one guilty, one acquitted). And the next day, I took a short flight from Amsterdam to London, and then rode a train south to a town called Farnborough. I was met at the station by a man named Mick Charles, the lead member of the British and American team whose job it had been to reconstruct Flight 103's fuselage in the months after the bombing. The remnants of the aircraft had been stored at Farnborough air base for more than ten years, but now that the trial was done, no one knew what would happen to them. Any relatives with an interest in seeing them were encouraged to make the trip after the verdict, so I did. I wanted to feel whatever it was I might be able to feel from those pieces of aluminium and plastic before they were moved to an aviation museum or sold for scrap.

Mick Charles took us, the relatives, to the high-security hangar. 'Here she is,' he said, walking up to the plane and touching the side as if he were visiting a horse in a stall. He reached up to a panel of aluminium that had been blown out from a centre point like the petals of a flower. 'The bomb exploded right here.' The aircraft was enormous, yet the amount of the original plane that was actually represented on that scaffolding was a small fraction. I had pictured an almost completely rebuilt 747 sitting in this hangar, with a cockpit, a tail, wings, engines, and seats – all I'd need to do was somehow put David back in his seat and the situation would be fixed.

Mick carried with him a seating chart for Flight 103. He said to a mother and son who were with me: 'You want to know his seat position, don't you?' I watched as he read out the seat number of the woman's husband and walked with her to the spot on the scaffolding where row 15 would have been. A few pieces of the plane's aluminium skin hung there, along with a small belt of windows. Mick was respectful of the relatives' relationship to the reconstructed fuselage. He offered to step outside if we wanted to be alone with it. I said yes without hesitation. The others left as I moved in close to the skin of the plane and touched it. Some dirt from the ground in Lockerbie was still on the underside. Some loose wiring and thin bits of insulation hung off the scaffolding. I had a sense that this was a last chance at something, and I didn't want to leave anything undone. I stood in the dark for a few seconds. It had been more than a dozen years since the bombing. What did this old wreck really matter to me?

There was no real connection between the way David had died and the way he had lived his life, even if some poetic interpretations suggested themselves; there was no meaning to a fall six miles down to the ground, just pain. It was terribly unfortunate that David chose to fly Pan Am Flight 103 on the 21st, but it wasn't a tragic choice to find the cheapest flight home. It wasn't a suicide. It was just what happened, and now I needed to be done with it. I walked outside, into the bright day, and Mick Charles shut off the lights in the hangar behind me. I wanted to go home.

Further reading

This extract from Ken Dornstein's book was published in a weekly news magazine called *The Week* (Dennis Publishing). This magazine is a superb way of staying in touch with the week's news and is ideal for Citizenship lessons and debating.

Once in a House on Fire

by Andrea Ashworth

In this extract, Andrea Ashworth writes powerfully about growing up in Manchester. A bright girl, she has to keep her head down at an unforgiving school and avoid the appalling routine violence of her stepfather (who she calls 'Dad') at home.

When it came to Parents' Evening, I was glad I had said nothing to make my teachers look down on Mum and Dad. Shame simmered in my veins, mingling with fiery pride, when I walked into the hall between them. Dad's neck was locked in a tie. My mother had applied a home perm; the curls were still coiled tight. She looked pretty but petrified.

'You both look fantastic,' I insisted. But there was no way they were going to step across the hall to meet Tamsyn's mother and father or any of the teachers. It was as if I was the parent and they were naughty children, hiding from the grown-ups.

'We weren't going to light up,' Dad whispered when I caught him and my mother rolling cigarettes behind a pillar in the hall: 'It's for when we get out of here.'

Miss Craig strode up and thrust out her hand to shake Dad's.

'Ahowd'yerdo?' He nearly choked over the aitch. The roll-up machine disappeared.

Miss Craig held my mother's hand for longer, looking her in the eye.

'I hope you realize what talent you've got on your hands.' She made it sound the opposite of a compliment. 'Andrea's a very gifted girl.'

Miss Craig urged them to send me to a good sixth-form college, to see that I read the papers – the broadsheets, she explained in a condescending[1] voice, such as *The Guardian*, *The Independent*, *The Times*, not the tabloids, like *The Sun* and the

---

[1]**condescending**   talking down to someone

Mirror. Not even the *Daily Express,* she made clear, when my mother wondered. Above all, they must ensure that I did my homework in quiet and peaceful surroundings.

'Your daughter is university material,' she said, before moving off to shake more hands: 'It would be criminal to let her abilities go to waste.'

'Snooty bitch!' Dad ground the gear stick into reverse, screeching out of the school car park. 'What've you been telling her, eh?'

'Nothing, Dad,' I swore.

'Miss Craig's always a bit high and mighty,' I tried to reassure my mother, who was still smarting from the snide[2] tone and innuendoes.[3] 'Everyone says so.'

I sat between my parents in the cab of our truck, my heart jiggling along, secretly memorizing everything Miss Craig had said. I had a chance – we jolted over bumps in the road – I had a chance. To get somewhere.

Though he had left school at fourteen, with not one qualification to his name, Dad made a point of exercising his grey matter every day by arguing with the headlines and editorial comments in *The Sun,* before moving on to the crossword, which, he was proud to admit, he always completed in record time. I would make him a cuppa, while he sweated over the puzzle. 'E-summat-A-F-summat-N-summat.' He would ponder a few seconds, caressing the barrel of his biro, before shoving all the clues aside to squeeze in his own wild words. I watched him wipe his brow, fill the boxes with a flourish, then sit back, satisfied – 'There we go: ELAFENT!'

When Dad had enjoyed his daily wrestle with the crossword and fallen into a snooze, I crept upstairs and spread the posh papers over my bedroom floor, where I set to with the scissors, to cut out items that I would paste into a scrapbook, the way

---

[2]**snide**   critical
[3]**innuendoes**   hints of criticism

Miss Craig had suggested. The miners were on strike. Precisely why the dispute could not be resolved, I was still not sure. Somehow Libya slipped into the equation: Arthur Scargill[4] visited Colonel Gadaffi[5] for tea, which involved armaments, money, promises. Trying to untangle Ireland and the IRA[6] was even more exasperating. I kept cutting and gluing, cutting and gluing, patching the world together.

On days when our house felt frighteningly brittle, it was consoling to go upstairs and turn the stuffed pages. Massacres and mangled bodies, explosions and mass drownings, gave me a terrible glow. It made me feel less alone, almost cosy, to see suffering splattered across the globe.

After school and on weekends, I used to lie on my bed for ages, letting pictures unroll inside my eyelids like a film. My future, a big house, full of lights, books lining the walls, swishy clothes, holidays in hot places, a lovely man, smiling . . .

The reel would snag and run out when Mum and Dad burst into screams or started banging around downstairs – slapping each other, knocking furniture over, threatening vile stuff. When they had had enough, the house would calm down to a murmur, the pair of them nursing their wounds over a pot of tea, talking about what was on telly, acting like nothing had happened. I would lie back on my bed, but my eyes would refuse to close. At times I could calm down by curling up, tucking my fists inside the cuffs of my jumper, pulling into myself.

Sometimes I got sick of waiting for my own life to start. The walls of our house felt as if they were closing in. It was hard to breathe. I was desperate to chisel the brace off my teeth, to let my mouth mingle with someone else's. Yet I knew that, even if my teeth were already straight, nothing romantic could happen

---

[4]**Arthur Scargill**   leader of the National Union of Mineworkers (NUM) from 1981 to 2000
[5]**Colonel Gadaffi**   the leader of Libya since 1969
[6]**IRA**   Irish Republican Army

to me while I lived at home. It was often sweetness and light: Mum lolling in Dad's lap, the two of them laughing and kissing, deep tongue kissing, while us kids tried to watch telly. But fights broke out so suddenly – spurting insults and fists, ashtrays flying – it wasn't safe to bring anyone in.

Further reading

In *Once in a House on Fire* (MacMillan Children's Books, 2004), Andrea Ashworth describes how she left a traumatic childhood behind, through education. Constance Briscoe, now a successful lawyer, tells a similar story in *Ugly* (Hodder & Stoughton Ltd, 2006). You might also like Barry Hines's famous novel, *A Kestrel for a Knave* (Penguin Books Ltd, 2000), which was made into the classic film *Kes*. For guidance about violence in the home, visit the Childline website: www.childline.org.uk

My Mam's Death

by Samantha Studley

In this short piece of autobiographical writing Samantha Studley thinks back to her memories of her mother's death, when she was just 14.

When I was fourteen and a half years old, my Mother (who was aged forty-two) died of cancer. At first, before she started to get really ill in December '82, my Dad had to get the doctor out to her. When the doctor came out he said that she would have to go into hospital for an operation on ulcers in her stomach, or so I thought anyway. She had the operation on 6 January 1983, and it turned out that she had cancer of the bowel. The doctor told my Dad that she would live for another year at the most.

She came through the operation quite well, which really built up my hopes that she'd pull through, because at the time I didn't know that she never had long to live. About two weeks after the operation, she got a bit better, talking, reading and just able to walk about a little bit. She came out of hospital in mid-February, and came home for a few weeks to stay with her Mother (my Gran) for rest and peace.

My Dad and my older brothers and sisters knew from the start she was dying, after the operation. Then just before she came back home to stay with us, my Dad gave me the shattering news about my Mam: 'Linda, I know I should have told you this a long time ago but your Mam's dying.' Just like that. I ran upstairs to my bedroom, and I broke down in tears. If he'd told me from the start, then I wouldn't have taken it so bad as I did. The few days after that, before Mam came out of hospital, were sheer hell, I just couldn't accept that my Mother was going to die, no way. She can't just leave me like that, after fourteen years with her as her daughter.

I couldn't wait for Mam to come home. I cleaned up the house from top to bottom, did the washing, ironing and made the beds so that the place would look spotless for her home-coming. I got flowers for her bedroom and the living room.

She came home just after Easter in 1983, and she was all right the first few days after coming home. I had to stay away (with special permission) from school to look after her, and my two-year-old brother Gerard (now four), while Dad went shopping.

In early May she gradually just got worse every day. She couldn't eat and had to stay in bed, wearing a colostomy bag.[1] All day and night she couldn't sleep and she kept taking tablets and pills all the time. I could hear her crying in the nights, which was the first time I'd ever heard her cry, and it used to break my heart. She lost loads of weight, and she couldn't walk. She was as thin as a matchstick and weighed about four stone. I used to look at her sitting in the chair like a vegetable, and she had to be carried everywhere. She couldn't go out anywhere, and because we had just got a new house, which should've been for Mam, she wanted to go and see it which was absolutely impossible for her because of her condition. Then in the early morning, about five a.m. on 2 June, she fell into a deep coma and after some final words she died at eight-thirty a.m. My life just fell apart. My Dad was a widower and my two-year-old brother was left (and me) to grow up without a mother.

After the death I just sat and moped about the house, lost weight, never ate much and I lost sleep. I stayed in every night for about a month, lost contact with all my friends, until my Dad encouraged me to go out again and face the world. I went to school the following week and gradually I picked up the shattered pieces of my torn apart life. My Mam was devoted to us, and she wanted my Dad to take great care of us.

She still remains in my life, because I'm part of her, and I shed a tear now and again for her.

---

[1]**colostomy bag**   a piece of the colon is diverted and human waste collected in a small bag outside the body

Further reading

Samantha Studley's text comes from a collection called *True to Life: Writings by Young Women* (Sheba Feminist Publishing, 1986). To read about a young woman growing up in Birmingham, read Meera Syal's hilarious and often moving *Anita and Me* (Flamingo, 1997).

Activities

If

Before you read

1   What do you know about the writer Rudyard Kipling? Spend some time finding out more about this influential writer. Write a paragraph summarising what you learn about him.

What's it about?

2   This is very clearly a poem giving advice.
  a   Write down three pieces of advice that the poem contains.
  b   Who is the advice aimed at? Make a list of the clues you find.

3   The poem is constructed around a series of opposites.
  a   Copy and complete the table below.

Statement	Opposite
trust yourself	
being lied about	
	risk it on one turn of pitch-and-toss
lose	
	keep your virtue
all men count with you	

  b   What overall impression does this use of opposites give? Look at these three statements and choose the one you think best sums up the poem's message:
  ● Do one thing, and don't do the opposite.
  ● Do one thing, but be prepared to do the opposite.
  ● Show balance by doing some of one thing but also some of the other.

  Discuss your ideas with the rest of your class.

Thinking about the text

4   The poem uses repetition to give impact to its message. Write down:
  a   what you notice about the repetition of words and phrases
  b   what effect you think this repetition has.

5   Take Rudyard Kipling's poem and convert it into a poster which gives the same advice in words and images for a modern audience. Make it eye-catching.

Through the Tunnel

Before you read

1 This story is set on a holiday. Think of your most memorable holiday. What were the best and worst parts of it? Why do you remember it so well? Draw a spider diagram to show the key features of the holiday.

What's it about?

Read the story and answer questions 2 and 3 by yourself. Then discuss your answers in a small group.

2 Using two columns, make a list of what we learn about Jerry and his mother during the story. Include details of:
   ● how they look and dress
   ● their background
   ● their relationship
   ● how they develop during the story.

3 'But he was happy. He was with them.' Why are the foreign boys so important to Jerry?
   a What do the foreign boys have that Jerry doesn't?
   b What does Jerry admire about the boys?
   c How does meeting the boys change Jerry's behaviour?

Thinking about the text

4 Look at the description of Jerry training hard and then finally swimming through the tunnel (from 'Jerry swam out to the big barrier rock' to 'He wanted nothing but to get back home and lie down'). Write down at least three words and phrases that Doris Lessing uses to show us that what Jerry is doing is difficult and dangerous, and comment on their effect on the reader.

5 Imagine you are Jerry looking back at the holiday as an adult. Write a diary entry in which you reflect on the impact of the experience. Ask yourself these questions and use your answers in your diary entry:
   ● What was the holiday like before you saw the foreign boys?
   ● Why were you so fascinated by the boys?
   ● Why were you determined to swim through the tunnel?
   ● How did you feel when you achieved your goal?
   ● How did the experience of swimming through the tunnel change you?

Almost Drowning

Before you read

1   Think of a time when something went wrong in your life. Perhaps you had an accident or suddenly found yourself in danger. How did you cope? How did the experience change you? Share your experience with a partner.

What's it about?

Read the extract and answer questions 2 and 3 by yourself. Then discuss your ideas in a small group.

2   **a**   Why do the Bransons choose Cozumel for their holiday?
    b   Why is Branson so keen to go fishing on that particular day?
    c   What does Branson mean when he says that the boat was 'in the eye of the storm'?
    d   Why does Branson feel uneasy about the fisherman cutting the line of the fish he has caught?
    e   What makes the Bransons decide to swim to shore rather than remain in the boat?

3   Working with a partner, write the script of a conversation between Richard and Kristen in which they talk about what happened to them, what they were thinking as the drama took place, and how they feel now the experience is behind them. Perform the conversation for another pair.

Thinking about the text

4   This extract describes a dramatic story. How does Richard Branson describe events? Is the tone of the extract dramatic, vivid or matter-of-fact? Write a short paragraph explaining how Branson chooses particular words and phrases to convey an atmosphere (you might look at the section where the fishermen and passengers realise that a storm is about to hit, for example), and comment on how effective you think his choices are.

5   What impression do you get of Richard Branson from this account? Choose three words to accurately describe how he feels at the end of the extract.

determined	*angry*	*upset*	*remorseful*	*guilty*
confused	*tough*	*foolhardy*	*bullying*	

Explain your choices to the rest of your class.

The Boy Who Fell out of the Sky

Before you read

1　As communication networks have improved, news has become more and more immediate. We hear about events very soon after they have happened – or even as they are happening. Older members of your family may well remember hearing or reading about the Lockerbie disaster the morning after it happened. Choose an event that everyone in your class remembers and discuss:

- where you were when you heard about the event
- what you remember about the event and how you heard about it
- the reactions of other people.

What's it about?

Read the extract and answer questions 2 and 3 by yourself. Then compare your answers with a partner's.

2　The extract describes a terrible event. Based on what Ken Dornstein tells us, what were the facts of the Lockerbie disaster?

3　The writer travels to the Netherlands to witness the trial of the suspected bombers, and to Britain to see the remains of the plane. Why is it important to him to make these journeys?

Thinking about the text

4　In some parts of the text, the writer uses very unemotional language, even though he is dealing with something very personal and upsetting. At others, his writing is very vivid and descriptive.

- **a**　Find at least three examples of surprisingly matter-of-fact language in the extract. Write a sentence or two explaining why you think Dornstein chooses to write in this way.
- **b**　Write down what you think Dornstein means by these phrases:
  - *a curtain dropping on my youth*
  - *a terrible storm that left me shipwrecked*

5　What overall impression do you get of Ken Dornstein? How has he been affected by the disaster? Discuss your ideas in a small group.

Once in a House on Fire

Before you read

1   Childhood can be a happy time, but also a time of cruelty and teasing. Think back to a time in your childhood when you fell out with friends or were teased. How did you feel? Write a paragraph describing the incident. Mention:
- how old you were
- what happened
- how you felt
- how things worked out.

What's it about?

Read the extract and answer questions 2 to 4 by yourself. Then compare your answers with a partner's.

2   What impression do you get of the writer from the extract – what is she like at the start and by the end?

3   The writer has very mixed feelings about her mother and step-father. Write down any clues in the text which show that either or both of her parents are:
a   nervous
b   trying their best to support Andrea
c   not familiar with how to behave in school
d   sometimes affectionate towards each other
e   sometimes violent.

4   What effect does the violence in her home have on Andrea Ashworth? How can you tell?

Thinking about the text

5   Look more closely at the first paragraph. What image does the writer's description create in your mind? Write a sentence or two explaining what the words in bold make you think of:
- *Shame **simmered** in my veins*
- ***fiery** pride*
- *Dad's neck was **locked** in a tie*

6   Andrea Ashworth says: 'Sometimes I got sick of waiting for my own life to start'. Imagine that you are interviewing her for your school magazine. What questions would you ask? Write up the interview.

My Mam's Death

Before you read

1   We all face bereavement in our lives – the death of people we love. Do you think schools could help pupils to cope with this experience? What could they do to help ease the pain? Write down three suggestions, then discuss your ideas with the rest of your class.

What's it about?

Read the extract and answer questions 2 and 3 by yourself. Then compare your answers with a partner's.

2   a   What were the signs of Samantha's mother's illness?
    b   How does Samantha's father react to his wife's illness?
    c   What was Samantha's mother like?

3   Which of these words do you think best sums up Samantha?

brave   frightened   worried   supportive
concerned   angry   confused

Write a sentence explaining your choice.

Thinking about the text

4   Look more closely at the language of the text. Write down an example of a very short sentence. Then write an example of a much longer, more breathless sentence. What effect do these different sentence lengths have?

5   Imagine that you are a friend of Samantha's and have recently read her account of her mother's death. Write a letter to her in which you:
    ● express your sympathy for what she is going through
    ● give her advice on how to cope with her emotions.

Compare and contrast

1   This section is called 'Facing the world'. It contains some texts showing people coping with demanding and stressful circumstances. Which text did you find the most interesting, and why? Write a short paragraph explaining your choice.

2   Some of the texts in this section are fiction (made-up stories) and some are based on real-life experiences. Think more about the difference between fiction and non-fiction texts by giving your response to these statements. For each one, decide whether you think the statement is:

   ● true (T)
   ● probably true (PT)
   ● probably not true (PNT)
   ● not true (NT).

   If you are not sure, put NS.

   a   Fiction texts such as *Through the Tunnel* help us to see into a person's mind and to understand their emotions more than non-fiction texts do.
   b   Non-fiction texts such as *The Boy Who Fell out of the Sky* are more powerful than fiction texts because we know the experience is real.
   c   Fiction texts use more description.
   d   Poems are better at showing emotions than facts.
   e   Texts that use first-person narration ('I') are more powerful than texts that use the third person ('he/she').

   Discuss your ideas in a small group.

3   Choose the central characters of two of the texts. Devise a chart or table to show in what ways they are similar and in what ways they are different. It might look like this:

	Person A	Person B
Ways in which they are similar		
Ways in which they are different		

4   Rudyard Kipling's poem at the start of the section gives advice. Based on your reading of at least three of the texts in the section, what do you think is the most important lesson people need to learn in order to survive the difficulties that life throws at us? Write a paragraph or two explaining your answer.

4 Britain in the past

This section explores some of our heritage – the events that make us who we are. In it you will learn about:

- what life would have been like if you had lived 1000 years ago
- what life was like for miners who spent their lives bent double underground
- what England was like during World War I.

The American thinker John W. Gardner said: 'History never looks like history when you are living through it.' With the world changing so rapidly, we can easily forget how we have been shaped by events of the past. This section gives some insights into what Britain was like – in the year 1000, in an age of war, at a time when men still worked all day and night in the coal mines.

Sometimes it is easy to forget how different life was for our ancestors. This section helps us to understand the world they lived in.

Activities

1   If time travel were possible, which period in British history would you be most interested to see as an eyewitness? Are there certain people, discoveries or events that you would choose? Here are some ideas:
    - the Roman occupation of Britain
    - the Industrial Revolution
    - different wars that have taken place
    - famous figures such as Elizabeth I and Winston Churchill
    - inventions such as the wheel, penicillin, steam engines, modernist painting.

    Choose a time, place, discovery or person you would like to visit as a time traveller. Then use a poster or paragraph to explain why – what would you hope to learn from the experience?

2   We sometimes assume that history happened a long time ago, in a different century. In fact, as John W. Gardner's quotation on page 107 reminds us, history is happening all the time and all around us. Interview someone in your family about how life was different for them when they were your age. Ask them about:
    ● their school life
    ● what technology they had – and didn't have (e.g. phones, computers, cars)
    ● what they ate
    ● how their social life was different.

    Present your findings in the form of a written or videoed interview called 'Life in the year XXXX'.

3   When you think back over your own life, what big events do you remember? Who are the people whom history will remember? Try to think of both good and bad events and people. Draw a chart or poster that captures the history that has happened during your life so far.

The Year 1000

by Robert Lacey and Danny Danziger

Former British Prime Minister Winston Churchill said: 'The further you look back, the further forward you are likely to see.' In other words, the past helps us to understand the present and the future.

Lacey and Danziger's book has a simple idea at its centre – to help us to see what life was like in the year 1000. This extract comes from the beginning of the book.

If you were to meet an Englishman in the year 1000, the first thing that would strike you would be how tall he was – very much the size of anyone alive today. It is generally believed that we are taller than our ancestors, and that is certainly true when we compare our stature to the size of more recent generations. Malnourished and overcrowded, the inhabitants of Georgian or Victorian England could not match our health or physique at the end of the twentieth century.

But the bones that have been excavated from the graves of people buried in England in the years around 1000 tell a tale of strong and healthy folk – the Anglo-Saxons who had occupied the greater part of the British Isles since the departure of the Romans. Nine out of ten of them lived in green and unpolluted countryside on a simple, wholesome diet that grew sturdy limbs – and very healthy teeth. It was during the centuries that followed the first millennium that overpopulation and overcrowding started to affect the stature and well-being of western Europeans. Excavations of later medieval sites reveal bodies that are already smaller than those discovered from the years around 1000, and archaeologists who have studied these centuries say that they can almost see the devastation of the Black Death[1] looming in the evidence of the increasingly frail and unhealthy skeletal remains.

---

[1]**Black Death**   a plague that afflicted Europe between 1347 and 1351, wiping out more than a third of the population

Life was simple. People wore the simple, sack-like tunics with leggings that we laugh at in the Monty Python movies, though in colours that were rather less muddy. Despite the lack of sharp chemical dyes in the year 1000, natural vegetable colourings could produce a range of strong and cheerful hues, with bright reds, greens, and yellows. It was a world without buttons, which had yet to be invented. Clothes were still fastened with clasps and thongs.

Life was short. A boy of twelve was considered old enough to swear an oath of allegiance to the king, while girls got married in their early teens, often to men who were significantly older than they were. Most adults died in their forties, and fifty-year-olds were considered venerable indeed. No one 'went out to work,' but the evidence of arthritis in the bones excavated from Anglo-Saxon graves indicates that most people endured a lifetime of hard manual labour – and the Julius Work Calendar[2] shows the different forms which that labour could take. Across the bottom of January's calendar page moves the ploughman, slicing open England's damp and often clay-ridden crust with the heavy iron blade that had been the making of the country's farming landscape.

'The ploughman feeds us all,' declared Aelfric, the Wessex schoolmaster who, in the years 987 to 1002, taught his pupils by getting them to observe and analyse the different economic activities they could see around them. 'The ploughman gives us bread and drink.'

It looks so slow and primitive to us, the heavy plough dragged by the oxen train. But compared to farming technologies in many other parts of the world at that time, the wheeled and iron-bladed plough of northwestern Europe was super-charged, enabling just two men to tear up a whole acre of soil with the help of the beasts which not only provided the 'horse-power' but enriched the fields with their manure.

---

[2]**Julius Work Calendar**   one of the earliest calendars, the Julius Work Calendar has a regular year of 365 days divided into 12 months, and a leap day is added to February every four years

The wheeled plough was the foundation of life for English people living in the year 1000. It opened the soil to air and water, enabling soluble minerals to reach deep levels, while rooting out weeds and tossing them aside to wither in the open air. It was not a new invention. In the middle of the first century AD, the Roman historian Pliny the Elder described some such device in use to the north of the Alps, and the evidence suggests that this powerful and handy machine was the crucial element in cultivating the land cleared from Europe's northwestern forests. One man to hold the plough, one to walk with the oxen, coaxing and singing and, when necessary, goading the animals forward with a stick: this drawing shows the furrows of freshly turned earth, the secret of how the soil had been tamed in the course of the previous centuries. It was the reason why, by the turn of the millennium, England was able to support a population of at least a million souls.

Further reading

If you enjoy reading entertaining history books, then you might also enjoy *1599: A Year in the Life of William Shakespeare* by James Shapiro (Faber and Faber, 2006). Compare it with a fictional account of Elizabethan England in Geoffrey Trease's fast-paced *Cue for Treason* (Puffin Books, 1973).

Down the Mine

by George Orwell

George Orwell was a well-known novelist and superb journalist, describing life in minute detail. Here he describes a working coal mine. Mining was once a major British industry, and miners worked long hours in dangerous conditions to bring coal to the surface.

When you go down a coal-mine it is important to try and get to the coal face when the 'fillers' are at work. This is not easy, because when the mine is working visitors are a nuisance and are not encouraged, but if you go at any other time, it is possible to come away with a totally wrong impression. On a Sunday, for instance, a mine seems almost peaceful. The time to go there is when the machines are roaring and the air is black with coal dust, and when you can actually see what the miners have to do. At those times the place is like hell, or at any rate like my own mental picture of hell. Most of the things one imagines in hell are there – heat, noise, confusion, darkness, foul air, and, above all, unbearably cramped space. Everything except the fire, for there is no fire down there except the feeble beams of Davy lamps and electric torches which scarcely penetrate the clouds of coal dust.

When you have finally got there – and getting there is a job in itself: I will explain that in a moment – you crawl through the last line of pit props and see opposite you a shiny black wall three or four feet high. This is the coal face. Overhead is the smooth ceiling made by the rock from which the coal has been cut; underneath is the rock again, so that the gallery you are in is only as high as the ledge of coal itself, probably not much more than a yard. The first impression of all, overmastering everything else for a while, is the frightful, deafening din from the conveyor belt which carries the coal away. You cannot see very far, because the fog of coal dust throws back the beam of your lamp, but you can see on either side of you the line of half-naked kneeling men, one to every four or five yards, driving their shovels under the fallen coal and flinging it swiftly over their left shoulders. They are feeding it on to the conveyor belt, a moving rubber belt a couple of feet wide which runs a yard or two behind them. Down this belt a glittering river of coal races constantly. In a big mine it is carrying away several tons of coal every minute. It bears it off to some place in the main roads where it is shot into tubs holding half a ton, and thence dragged to the cages and hoisted to the outer air.

It is impossible to watch the 'fillers' at work without feeling a pang of envy for their toughness. It is a dreadful job that they do, an almost superhuman job by the standard of an ordinary person. For they are not only shifting monstrous quantities of coal, they are also doing it in a position that doubles or trebles the work. They have got to remain kneeling all the while – they could hardly rise from their knees without hitting the ceiling – and you can easily see by trying it what a tremendous effort this means. Shovelling is comparatively easy when you are standing up, because you can use your knee and thigh to drive the shovel along; kneeling down, the whole of the strain is thrown upon

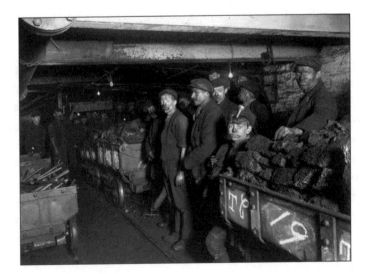

your arm and belly muscles. And the other conditions do not exactly make things easier. There is the heat – it varies, but in some mines it is suffocating – and the coal dust that stuffs up your throat and nostrils and collects along your eyelids, and the unending rattle of the conveyor belt, which in that confined space is rather like the rattle of a machine gun. But the fillers look and work as though they were made of iron. They really do look like iron – hammered iron statues – under the smooth coat of coal dust which clings to them from head to foot. It is only when you see miners down the mine and naked that you realize what splendid men they are. Most of them are small (big men are at a disadvantage in that job) but nearly all of them have the most noble bodies; wide shoulders tapering to slender supple waists, and small pronounced buttocks and sinewy[1] thighs, with not an ounce of waste flesh anywhere. In the hotter mines they wear only a pair of thin drawers, clogs and knee-pads; in the hottest mines of all, only the clogs and knee-pads. You can hardly tell by the look of them whether they are young or old. They may be any age up to sixty or even sixty-five, but when they are black and naked they all look alike. No one could do their work who had not a young man's body, and a figure fit for a guardsman at that; just a few pounds of extra flesh on the waist-line, and the constant bending would be impossible. You can never forget that spectacle once you have seen it – the line of bowed, kneeling figures, sooty black all over, driving their huge shovels under the coal with stupendous force and speed. They are on the job for seven and a half hours, theoretically without a break, for there is no time 'off'. Actually they snatch a quarter of an hour or so at some time during the shift to eat the food they have brought with them, usually a hunk of bread and dripping and a bottle of cold tea. The first time I was watching the 'fillers' at work I put my hand upon some dreadful slimy thing among the coal dust. It was a chewed quid of tobacco. Nearly all the miners chew tobacco, which is said to be good against thirst.

---

[1]**sinewy**   strong and wiry

Probably you have to go down several coal-mines before you can get much grasp of the processes that are going on round you. This is chiefly because the mere effort of getting from place to place makes it difficult to notice anything else. In some ways it is even disappointing, or at least is unlike what you have expected. You get into the cage, which is a steel box about as wide as a telephone box and two or three times as long. It holds ten men, but they pack it like pilchards in a tin, and a tall man cannot stand upright in it. The steel door shuts upon you, and somebody working the winding gear above drops you into the void. You have the usual momentary qualm in your belly and a bursting sensation in the ears, but not much sensation of movement till you get near the bottom, when the cage slows down so abruptly that you could swear it is going upwards again. In the middle of the run the cage probably touches sixty miles an hour; in some of the deeper mines it touches even more. When you crawl out at the bottom you are perhaps four hundred yards underground. That is to say you have a tolerable-sized mountain on top of you; hundreds of yards of solid rock, bones of extinct beasts, subsoil, flints, roots of growing things, green grass and cows grazing on it – all this suspended over your head and held back only by wooden props as thick as the calf of your leg. But because of the speed at which the cage has brought you down, and the complete blackness through which you have travelled, you hardly feel yourself deeper down than you would at the bottom of the Piccadilly tube.[2]

What *is* surprising, on the other hand, is the immense horizontal distances that have to be travelled underground. Before I had been down a mine I had vaguely imagined the miner stepping out of the cage and getting to work on a ledge of coal a few yards away. I had not realized that before he even gets to work he may have had to creep along passages as long as from

---

[2]**Piccadilly tube**   a London underground railway line from the north-east to the west of London

London Bridge to Oxford Circus. In the beginning, of course, a mine shaft is sunk somewhere near a seam of coal. But as that seam is worked out and fresh seams are followed up, the workings get further and further from the pit bottom. If it is a mile from the pit bottom to the coal face, that is probably an average distance; three miles is a fairly normal one; there are even said to be a few mines where it is as much as five miles. But these distances bear no relation to distances above ground. For in all that mile or three miles as it may be, there is hardly anywhere outside the main road, and not many places even there, where a man can stand upright.

You do not notice the effect of this till you have gone a few hundred yards. You start off, stooping slightly, down the dim-lit gallery, eight or ten feet wide and about five high, with the walls built up with slabs of shale, like the stone walls in Derbyshire. Every yard or two there are wooden props holding up the beams and girders; some of the girders have buckled into fantastic curves under which you have to duck. Usually it is bad going underfoot – thick dust or jagged chunks of shale, and in some mines where there is water it is as mucky as a farm-yard. Also there is the track for the coal tubs, like a miniature railway track with sleepers a foot or two apart, which is tiresome to walk on. Everything is grey with shale dust; there is a dusty fiery smell which seems to be the same in all mines. You see mysterious machines of which you never learn the purpose, and bundles of tools slung together on wires, and sometimes mice darting away from the beam of the lamps. They are surprisingly common, especially in mines where there are or have been horses. It would be interesting to know how they got there in the first place; possibly by falling down the shaft – for they say a mouse can fall any distance uninjured, owing to its surface area being so large relative to its weight. You press yourself against the wall to make way for lines of tubs jolting slowly towards the shaft, drawn by an endless steel cable operated from the surface. You creep through sacking curtains and thick wooden doors which, when they are opened, let out fierce blasts of air. These doors are an important part of the ventilation system. The exhausted air is sucked out of one shaft by means of fans, and the fresh air enters the other of its own accord. But if left to itself the air will take the shortest way round, leaving the deeper workings unventilated; so all the short cuts have to be partitioned off.

At the start to walk stooping is rather a joke, but it is a joke that soon wears off. I am handicapped by being exceptionally tall, but when the roof falls to four feet or less it is a tough job for anybody except a dwarf or a child. You not only have to bend double, you have also got to keep your head up all the while so as to see the beams and girders and dodge them when they come. You have, therefore, a constant crick in the neck, but this is nothing to the pain in your knees and thighs. After half a mile it becomes (I am not exaggerating) an unbearable agony. You begin to wonder whether you will ever get to the end – still more, how on earth you are going to get back. Your pace grows slower and slower. You come to a stretch of a couple of hundred yards where it is all exceptionally low and you have to work yourself along in a squatting position. Then suddenly the roof opens out to a mysterious height – scene of an old fall of rock, probably – and for twenty whole yards you can stand upright. The relief is overwhelming. But after this there is another low stretch of a hundred yards and then a succession of beams which you have to crawl under. You go down on all fours; even this is a relief after the squatting business. But when you come to the end of the beams and try to get up again, you find that your knees have temporarily struck work and refuse to lift you. You call a halt, ignominiously,[3] and say that you would like to rest for a minute or two. Your guide (a miner) is sympathetic. He knows that your muscles are not the same as his. 'Only another four hundred yards,' he says encouragingly; you feel that he might as well say another four hundred miles. But finally you do somehow creep as far as the coal face. You have

---

[3]**ignominiously**   with a feeling of shame

gone a mile and taken the best part of an hour; a miner would do it in not much more than twenty minutes. Having got there, you have to sprawl in the coal dust and get your strength back for several minutes before you can even watch the work in progress with any kind of intelligence.

Coming back is worse than going, not only because you are already tired out but because the journey back to the shaft is slightly uphill. You get through the low places at the speed of a tortoise, and you have no shame now about calling a halt when your knees give way. Even the lamp you are carrying becomes a nuisance and probably when you stumble you drop it; whereupon, if it is a Davy lamp, it goes out. Ducking the beams becomes more and more of an effort, and sometimes you forget to duck. You try walking head down as the miners do, and then you bang your backbone. Even the miners bang their backbones fairly often. This is the reason why in very hot mines, where it is necessary to go about half naked, most of the miners have what they call 'buttons down the back' – that is, a permanent scab on each vertebra. When the track is downhill the miners sometimes fit their clogs, which are hollow underneath, on to the trolley rails and slide down. In mines where the 'travelling' is very bad all the miners carry sticks about two and a half feet long, hollowed out below the handle. In normal places you keep your hand on top of the stick and in the low places you slide your hand down into the hollow. These sticks are a great help, and the wooden crash-helmets – a comparatively recent invention – are a godsend. They look like a French or Italian steel helmet, but they are made of some kind of pith and very light, and so strong that you can take a violent blow on the head without feeling it. When finally you get back to the surface you have been perhaps three hours underground and travelled two miles, and you are more exhausted than you would be by a twenty-five-mile walk above ground. For a week afterwards your thighs are so stiff that coming downstairs is quite a difficult feat; you have to work your way down in a peculiar sidelong manner, without bending the knees. Your miner friends notice the stiffness of your walk and chaff you about it. ('How'd ta like to work down pit, eh?' etc.) Yet even a miner who has been long away from work – from illness, for instance – when he comes back to the pit, suffers badly for the first few days.

It may seem that I am exaggerating, though no one who has been down an old-fashioned pit (most of the pits in England are old-fashioned) and actually gone as far as the coal face, is likely to say so. But what I want to emphasize is this. Here is this frightful business of crawling to and fro, which to any normal person is a hard day's work in itself; and it is not part of the miner's work at all, it is merely an extra, like the City man's daily ride in the Tube.

Further reading

George Orwell's most famous and disturbing novels are *Animal Farm* (Penguin Books Ltd, 2000) and *Nineteen Eighty-Four* (Penguin Books Ltd, 2004). If you like non-fiction accounts of life in England over the past 2000 years, try *England: The Autobiography* (edited by John Lewis-Stempel, Penguin Books Ltd, 2006), which contains a host of fascinating eyewitness accounts of historical events.

The Village Blacksmith

by Henry Wadsworth Longfellow

Henry Wadsworth Longfellow was an American poet who lived for most of his life in Cambridge, Massachusetts. This poem describes a way of life that has now almost died out.

Under a spreading chestnut tree
    The village smithy[1] stands;
The smith, a mighty man is he,
    With large and sinewy hands;
And the muscles of his brawny arms
    Are strong as iron bands.

His hair is crisp, and black, and long,
    His face is like the tan;[2]
His brow is wet with honest sweat,
    He earns whate'er he can,
And looks the whole world in the face,
    For he owes not any man.

Week in, week out, from morn till night,
    You can hear his bellows blow;
You can hear him swing his heavy sledge,
    With measured beat and slow,
Like a sexton[3] ringing the village bell,
    When the evening sun is low.

---

[1]**smithy**   blacksmith's workshop
[2]**tan**   leather
[3]**sexton**   someone who looks after a churchyard, including ringing the bells

And children coming home from school
   Look in at the open door;
They love to see the flaming forge,
   And hear the bellows roar,
And catch the burning sparks that fly
   Like chaff from a threshing floor.

He goes on Sunday to the church,
   And sits among his boys;
He hears the parson pray and preach,
   He hears his daughter's voice,
Singing in the village choir,
   And it makes his heart rejoice.

It sounds to him like her mother's voice,
   Singing in Paradise!
He needs must think of her once more,
   How in the grave she lies;
And with his hard, rough hand he wipes
   A tear out of his eyes.

Toiling, – rejoicing, – sorrowing,
   Onward through life he goes;
Each morning sees some task begin,
   Each evening sees it close;
Something attempted, something done,
   Has earned a night's repose.

Thanks, thanks to thee, my worthy friend,
   For the lesson thou hast taught!
Thus at the flaming forge of life
   Our fortunes must be wrought;
Thus on its sounding anvil shaped
   Each burning deed and thought!

Further reading

To learn more about village life in England in the past, read Ronald Blythe's *Akenfield* (Penguin Books Ltd, 2005) – an account of rural traditions in Suffolk. For powerful and often disturbing poetry about nature, see Ted Hughes's *Collected Poems* (Faber and Faber, 2005).

MCMXIV[1]

by Philip Larkin

In 1914 Europe was torn apart by World War I. Philip Larkin's poem paints a picture of the days before the war broke out, with many young Englishmen queuing patiently to join the army. Writing more than 50 years later, Philip Larkin tries to imagine what life felt like then.

Those long uneven lines
Standing as patiently
As if they were stretched outside
The Oval[2] or Villa Park,[3]
The crowns of hats, the sun
On moustached archaic[4] faces
Grinning as if it were all
An August Bank Holiday lark;[5]

[1]**MCMXIV**   1914, expressed in Roman numerals
[2]**The Oval**   cricket ground in London
[3]**Villa Park**   football ground in Birmingham, England
[4]**archaic**   very old
[5]**lark**   joke

And the shut shops, the bleached
Established names on the sunblinds,
The farthings and sovereigns,
And dark-clothed children at play
Called after kings and queens,
The tin advertisements
For cocoa and twist,[6] and the pubs
Wide open all day;

And the countryside not caring:
The place-names all hazed over
With flowering grasses, and fields
Shadowing Domesday[7] lines;
Under wheat's restless silence;
The differently dressed servants
With tiny rooms in huge houses,
The dust behind limousines;

Never such innocence,
Never before or since,
As changed itself to past
Without a word – the men
Leaving the gardens tidy,
The thousands of marriages
Lasting a little while longer:
Never such innocence again.

---

[6]**twist**   tobacco
[7]**Domesday**   the Domesday Book was started in 1081 by William I; it showed
    in detail how the land of England was organised and who it belonged to

Further reading

If you'd like to read more by Philip Larkin, try his *Collected Poems* (Faber and Faber, 2003). If you are specifically interested in texts from World War I, see *Voices of the Great War* (edited by Geoff Barton; Longman, 1997).

The Roses of No Man's Land

by Lyn MacDonald

There are some aspects of World War I that many people know very little about. One of these is the work of what Lyn MacDonald calls 'The Roses of No Man's Land'. These are the nurses who worked at the front line and in the hospitals back home during the war. They had to deal with some of the most appalling injuries ever seen, caused by the new technology of the war, and with medicines and methods that today seem to us very limited. In this extract from her historical account (taken from chapters one and two), Lyn MacDonald uses her own research plus the voices of people who were in the war to describe what it was like.

It was exactly one week since the ringing of church bells had mingled with the first shots in the battle of Mons, and seventeen days since the first contingents of the BEF[1] had been happily basking in a heroes' welcome. Of the 90,000 men who had landed in France, one in every six had become a casualty. The ranks of the BEF were horribly depleted and before many more days had passed, its remnants would be fighting shoulder to shoulder with its French allies in the battle of the Marne.

The Germans were almost at the gates of Paris, but in the hospital which had been hastily set up in the Grand Trianon Hotel at Versailles, the doctors and nurses had little time to brood on the progress of the war. What worried them a great deal more was the unprecedented character of the wounds they were trying to treat – almost all of them infected with gas gangrene.

Captain Geoffrey Keynes, RAMC

We knew nothing about it at all. Nothing like it had ever been experienced in South Africa on the clean, sandy battleground of the

---

[1]**BEF**   British Expeditionary Force; another name for the British army sent to France and Belgium during World War I

*veldt, which had been the army's last experience. Here, on the heavily
manured soil of France, it was a different matter. You got this appalling
infection with anaerobic[2] bacteria and the men just died like flies. We
got the casualties straight from Mons and the infection had usually set
in by the time they got to us. If they had compound fractures, full of
mud, it was the ideal site for the bacteria to flourish, and, if the men
had been several days on the way, as most of them had, the wound was
simply a mass of putrid muscle rotting with gas gangrene. Nothing to
do with gas as we knew it later in the war. It was called that because the
bacillus that grows in the wound creates gas. The whole thing balloons
up. You can tap it under your fingers and it sounds hollow. Even with
quite a slight wound, when soil and shreds of uniform are carried in by
the missile, it starts up. They soon died. We simply didn't know how to
treat it. We'd never come across it before. Of course, there were no
antibiotics.[3] No effective disinfectants. We would cut away as much of
the diseased tissue as we could. On a leg or an arm we would remove
the limb, but that didn't stop it. It just went on up, and still the men
would die from the toxic effects of the products of the bacteria. That was
the worst thing in the first few months of the war.*

Already, the doctors had an inkling that this was to be a different kind of war, and it was a suspicion that the army commanders were beginning to share. Like Le Cateau and the actions on the Marne and the Aisne, the action at Mons[4] clearly demonstrated to British, French and Germans alike that the technical development of modern weaponry had rendered completely useless the old methods of attack, and with them all the military ideas which had governed warfare and training for half a millennium.

It was a lesson they were slow to learn. After four years of bitter contemplation, Field-Marshal Lord French wrote with admirable candour:[5]

---

[2]**anaerobic**   grows without air
[3]**antibiotics**   modern medicines that destroy micro-organisms
[4]**Le Cateau, the Marne, the Aisne, Mons**   sites of major battles in France
[5]**candour**   openness

It is easy to be 'wise after the event'; but I cannot help wondering why none of us realized what the modern rifle, the machine-gun, motor traction, the aeroplane and wireless telegraphy would bring about. It seems so simple when judged by actual results ... All my thoughts, all my prospective plans, all my possible alternatives of action were concentrated upon a war of movement and manoeuvre.

Field-Marshal Viscount French of Ypres, 1914

By November 1914, their strategy defeated by the deadliness of their own weapons, the opposing armies had ground to a halt, each entrenched in a fixed position which, give or take a mile or so, would hardly alter for the next three and a half years. Already, two-thirds of Europe was alight, and the flames were licking outwards to engulf half the world. Years later, when they struck the medals, they called it The Great War for Civilization. The truth was that Civilization would never be quite the same again.

There was hardly a hint, in that golden summer of 1914, that the world was about to come to an end.

The great British lion, basking at the heart of its Empire, gave the slightest twitch of its ears at the echo of a double pistol shot far away in the Balkans.[6] But on that summer Sunday when the Austrian Archduke Ferdinand[7] was assassinated at Sarajevo, the anxieties of politically conscious people were concentrated on Ireland, where there was a real risk of civil war.

The weather was beautiful. Garden parties, tennis parties, village fêtes could all be looked forward to in the happy certainty that the sun would co-operate. No 'best hats' would wilt in the damp. Picnics would not be rained off. No sudden showers would interrupt the delicate flirtations of couples strolling discreetly in shrubberies within earshot of lawns and tennis courts where middle-aged ladies, heads bobbing under

---

[6]**the Balkans**   south-eastern Europe, including countries such as Turkey, Bulgaria and Serbia
[7]**Austrian Archduke Ferdinand**   the assassination of the leader of Austria in 1914 triggered World War I

silk sunshades, cluck-clucked together over the free and easy behaviour of the modern generation.

In its own eyes it was a startlingly modern generation. Born in the last decade of the nineteenth century, in their brief lifetime twenty-year-olds had seen the horse make way for the motor car, gaslight ousted by electricity, the telephone become an almost everyday convenience, and, if aeroplanes were not exactly commonplace, they no longer caused neck-craning crowds to gather as they had done a decade earlier. Every drawing-room and all but the poorest front parlours still boasted a piano, but the old parlour songs had long ago been relegated to the recesses of piano stools. It was ragtime that stood on the music stands, and ragtime that caused parents to cover their ears as it jangled from the horns of the newfangled gramophones, beloved by the young.

'Hitchy koo, hitchy koo, hitchy koo,' they sang, as they two-stepped to the tinkling of the latest hit. 'Oh, you *beautiful* doll,' warbled young men, gazing meaningfully into the eyes of pretty partners. 'Hello, hello, who's your lady friend?' enquired more robustly melodious crowds, free and easy on day trips to the sea.

But in spite of their up-to-date ideas, in spite of their easy acceptance of mechanical toys and scientific advances, and in spite of an awakening social conscience far removed from the soup-kitchen philosophy of their Victorian parents, the roots of the young generation were still firmly embedded in the Victorian age into which they had been born. It was to that high noon of power and Empire, of prosperity and expansion, of national pride and security, that they owed their unshakeable confidence, their patriotism and the unquestioning sense of duty that went with it.

It was pleasant to be newly grown up. Girls of the élite were presented at Court and admitted to the butterfly social round. Girls of the working class merely exchanged the discipline of the classroom for the factory bench, the sewing machine or the drudgery of domestic service. For the daughters of the industrious professional and businessmen who made up the middle classes, 'growing up' meant putting down their skirts, putting up their hair and 'coming out' at whatever local dance happened to take place nearest to their eighteenth birthdays. Kit Dodsworth, daughter of a Yorkshire lawyer, was typical of her generation.

Kit Dodsworth

We were terribly strictly brought up. Until I was eighteen, I lived up in the schoolroom. If the grown-ups had a tennis party we were allowed to come down and field the balls for them, but we had to go back to the schoolroom for tea and then go down again. We never met anyone, and I was petrified with shyness.

I came out at a big dance. It was the Yorkshire Hussars Ball, and I had a marvellous dress. It was white satin, all beaded. It cost twelve pounds – and that was a frightful price! After that one evening you were grown up; until then you were a child.

We lived very comfortably with lots of servants, so there was no real work to do. We tidied our rooms. We paid calls; we had tea-parties; we sewed; we taught at Sunday School; we organized bazaars and fêtes, made sweets and cakes for them. We always seemed to be busy.

Even with an abundance of servants, there was plenty to do in the home. Some girls, more adventurous or more persistent, bored with the small-change of domestic life, succeeded in cajoling parents into allowing them to take up a career. Nursing and teaching were acceptable, and social work was not frowned on so long as it was unpaid. But the universal attitude was that girls who didn't need to work should not take jobs away from those who did.

Hilda and Gladys Pole, the youngest of the five daughters of a clergyman in Kent, just back from six absorbing months at finishing school in Stuttgart, settled down to enjoy the social life of Chislehurst, and to help their mother and elder sisters. They joined the Red Cross because it was regarded as the sensible thing to do.

Girls who were unlikely ever to have to light a fire, cook a meal or sweep a floor would nevertheless, in their future married state, have to cope with illness, to deal with household accidents and eventually to nurse children ailing with the unavoidable fevers and infectious diseases which no amount of comfortable prosperity could prevent and only careful nursing could cure. So they joined the Red Cross or St John Ambulance Brigade, met their friends at the sociable weekly classes, did a little studying and sat the exams. The First Aid Certificate qualified them to dress cuts and grazes and bandage broken limbs. The Home Nursing Certificate demanded proficiency in the elementary skills of smoothing pillows, making beds and concocting beef tea. It was laudable as well as useful. Best of all, it was a sociable afternoon out. Kit Dodsworth was motivated less by the cause of suffering humanity than by the fact that she had a crush on a local doctor who gave occasional lectures. Millicent Norton found it a heaven-sent excuse to spend two afternoons a week out of the house, away from the baleful[8] gaze of a repressive[9] father who had failed to notice the ending of the prudish Victorian era thirteen years earlier.

Millicent Norton, later Commandant of Sussex 66 VAD Convalescent Hospital

My father was old. He was nearly seventy when I was twenty, and very, very old-fashioned. My sister and I were both terrified of my father. You never dared go against your parents. After I left school, a friend asked me to go and stay with her family in Ireland, and by some miracle my mother managed to persuade Father to let me go. When I got to the station I discovered that he had brought his own luggage with him. I simply couldn't believe it. He said, 'You don't think I'd be letting you go alone, do you? I am coming over too. I have booked into a hotel opposite their house.' I shall never forget how embarrassed I was, having to explain that my father had come too. Of course, they were very polite and said, 'Well, do ask him to call.' But he wouldn't. He just stood at the window of this hotel. We could see him watching us every time we went out.

---

[8]**baleful**   gloomy, threatening
[9]**repressive**   restricting

Further reading

Lyn MacDonald has written various fascinating books about World War I. All contain eyewitness accounts which she has collected by talking to survivors of the war. You might start with *1914: The Days of Hope* (Penguin Books Ltd, 1989). One of the most powerful novels about life in the War is Sebastian Faulks's *Birdsong* (Vintage, 1999).

Not My Best Side

by U. A. Fanthorpe

(Uccello: *Saint George and the Dragon*, The National Gallery)

U. A. Fanthorpe is a former teacher who is well known for her poetry. She quite often writes using the voices of characters, and shows their different perspectives. This poem is about Saint George (born c.275, died 23 April 303), a soldier of the Roman Empire who became a saint after being tortured to death for confessing himself a Christian. He was glorified in the tale of George and the Dragon, and is the patron saint of several countries and cities, including England, Georgia, Barcelona and Moscow.

The poem tells the story of his encounter with the dragon based on the famous painting by Uccello (1397–1475), a Florentine painter who was fascinated by perspective in art. This helped him to create a feeling of depth in his paintings.

I

Not my best side, I'm afraid.
The artist didn't give me a chance to
Pose properly, and as you can see,
Poor chap, he had this obsession with
Triangles, so he left off two of my
Feet. I didn't comment at the time
(What, after all, are two feet
To a monster?) but afterwards
I was sorry for the bad publicity.
Why, I said to myself, should my conqueror
Be so ostentatiously[1] beardless, and ride
A horse with a deformed neck and square hoofs?
Why should my victim be so
Unattractive as to be inedible,[2]
And why should she have me literally

---

[1] **ostentatiously**   very obviously, so that it attracts people's attention
[2] **inedible**   impossible to eat

On a string? I don't mind dying
Ritually, since I always rise again,
But I should have liked a little more blood
To show they were taking me seriously.

II

It's hard for a girl to be sure if
She wants to be rescued. I mean, I quite
Took to the dragon. It's nice to be
Liked, if you know what I mean. He was
So nicely physical, with his claws
And lovely green skin, and that sexy tail,
And the way he looked at me,
He made me feel he was all ready to
Eat me. And any girl enjoys that.
So when this boy turned up, wearing machinery,
On a really *dangerous* horse, to be honest,
I didn't much fancy him. I mean,
What was he like underneath the hardware?
He might have acne, blackheads or even
Bad breath for all I could tell, but the dragon –
Well, you could see all his equipment
At a glance. Still, what could I do?
The dragon got himself beaten by the boy,
And a girl's got to think of her future.

III

I have diplomas in Dragon
Management and Virgin Reclamation.
My horse is the latest model, with
Automatic transmission and built-in
Obsolescence.[3] My spear is custom-built,
And my prototype armour
Still on the secret list. You can't
Do better than me at the moment.

---

[3]**obsolescence**   loss of usefulness

I'm qualified and equipped to the
Eyebrow. So why be difficult?
Don't you want to be killed and/or rescued
In the most contemporary[4] way? Don't
You want to carry out the roles
That sociology[5] and myth[6] have designed for you?
Don't you realize that, by being choosy,
You are endangering job-prospects
In the spear- and horse-building industries?
What, in any case, does it matter what
You want? You're in my way.

Further reading

If you liked this, try some of U. A. Fanthorpe's other poems in *Collected Poems 1978–2003* (Peterloo Poets, 2005). For a factual account of Saint George, read Anita Ganeri's *The Life of St George* (Heinemann Library, 2005).

---

[4]**contemporary**   modern
[5]**sociology**   the study of how society works
[6]**myth**   old stories which may or may not be true

Activities

The Year 1000

Before you read

1   Some politicians say that History should be a compulsory subject all the way through school to the age of 16. They say that it's so important, everyone should study it. Working with a partner, think about whether you agree or disagree. Using two columns, make a list of the arguments for and against having History as a core subject. Discuss your conclusions with the rest of your class.

What's it about?

Read the extract and answer questions 2 to 4 by yourself. Then compare your answers with a partner's.

2   This extract is full of facts. Write down what you have learned about life in the year 1000.
   a   How tall were the people?
   b   Where did 90% of the people live?
   c   Write down a word that describes what people's teeth were like.
   d   Write down one item of clothing that people wore.
   e   What was the average lifespan of people?
   f   How many people were there in England?

3   Why did the plough prove to be such an important invention?

4   Write down three positive aspects and two negative aspects of life in the year 1000.

Thinking about the text

5   Look again at the first two paragraphs of the text. The authors use some complex vocabulary (such as 'malnourished', 'inhabitants', 'unpolluted', 'millennium'). Rewrite the first two paragraphs for readers aged 7–11: simplify the words and try to make the meaning really clear.

6   Imagine what life might have been like for someone of your age in the year 1000. Write a diary entry describing what you do during one day. Use information from the text to guide you. Make your entry as interesting and entertaining as possible. You could start like this:
   Just back from the fields . . .

Down the Mine

Before you read

1   What do you already know about how coal was mined from beneath the surface of the earth in Britain? What did miners actually do? Which areas of Britain had the most mines? Working in a small group, use a spider diagram to brainstorm what you know about Britain's mining industry.

What's it about?

Read the text and answer questions 2 and 3 by yourself. Then compare your answers with a partner's.

2   Examine the way the text is written.
   a   Find an example of a *fact* from the text and write it down.
   b   Find an example of an *opinion* expressed by George Orwell.
   c   How would you describe Orwell's attitude to what he witnesses? Choose the word you think is most appropriate:

shocked	*fascinated*	*appalled*	*disturbed*
happy	*curious*	*outraged*	

   Find a sentence in the text that supports your choice. What words and phrases does Orwell use to convey his feelings?

3   How is life down the mine different from what you might have expected?

Thinking about the text

4   The extract shows what work was like for some people in the past – hard, physical, dangerous and often brutal. Working in a group of three, put together an interview with a miner and a member of his family (e.g. his wife or child) in which you find out more about what it was like to be a miner and to be part of a miner's family. Perform your interview for the rest of your class.

5   George Orwell's account was written many years ago. If he was writing today, would he use different language? Imagine you are writing a newspaper article about visiting a mine. Write the opening two or three paragraphs. Then write two or three sentences explaining how your language is different from Orwell's.

The Village Blacksmith

Before you read

1 This poem is about a job that has almost died out now – that of the blacksmith. Working with a partner, brainstorm some other jobs that no longer exist in everyday life. See if you can think of three to five jobs.

What's it about?

2 The poem gives a detailed portrait of the blacksmith, where he works and what he looks like. Read the poem and then draw a diagram. Label it with details about the blacksmith, his tools and where he works.

3 What do other people think of the blacksmith?
   a Write down three things that the village children like about the blacksmith.
   b Write down two things that the narrator of the poem admires about him.

4 Write down what you think the writer means when he writes:

   [He] looks the whole world in the face, / For he owes not any man.

   Explain what you understand this to mean by putting it into your own words.

Thinking about the text

5 Look at the last verse of the poem. The last four lines are a metaphor (an idea or image that stands for something else). What do the images in these lines stand for? What is the 'lesson' that the blacksmith has taught? In a small group, discuss what you think is the meaning of this last verse.

6 The village blacksmith was an important part of village life in the 19th century. Write a short magazine article in which you interview the blacksmith about what his life is like.

MCMXIV

Before you read

1   What do you already know about World War I? For example:
-   Why was it a 'world war'?
-   Why do people sometimes refer to it as 'the Great War'?
-   What forms of fighting were involved?
-   What caused the war and how did it end?
-   What impact did the war have on those who fought in it – how many died and how were the survivors affected?

Working in a small group, use a spider diagram to note down everything you know about the war.

What's it about?

2   The poem is about England on the brink of World War I. Read it all the way through, then look again at the first verse. Find two phrases that Philip Larkin uses to suggest that the people do not realise the seriousness of their situation.

3   Many people think that this poem is typically English. Write down three points from the poem that seem to you typical of what England used to be like.

Thinking about the text

4   Philip Larkin is known for his interesting use of language. Write down the image each of these phrases creates in your mind:
-   *moustached archaic faces*
-   *the countryside not caring*
-   *wheat's restless silence.*

5   Many men enlisted to go to war, full of pride and enthusiasm. Some of those who returned told tales of terrible suffering. Working with a partner, devise an interview with one of the people described in the poem as lining up patiently to go to war. Find out more about why he volunteered, what he hoped to achieve, and how he felt on that summer's day. You might then ask about how he feels now the war is over. Perform your interview for the rest of your class.

The Roses of No Man's Land

Before you read

1 Being a doctor or nurse can be a gory and upsetting job. List what you think are the good and bad parts of the job. Do you think your list would have been different if you had been writing it during World War I? Discuss your ideas with the rest of your class.

What's it about?

Read the extract and answer questions 2 and 3 by yourself. Then compare your answers with a partner's.

2 What do we learn about the conditions in the hospitals during the war from the different accounts given in the extract? For each of the main eyewitnesses (Captain Geoffrey Keynes, Lord French, Kit Dodsworth and Millicent Norton), write down three things you have learned about the conditions in the hospitals and the war generally.

3 Look again at Lyn MacDonald's text. Write down an example of:
   ● a factual statement
   ● a personal feeling
   ● a statement that makes life in 1914 seem very different from life today
   ● a statement that could just as easily have been written about life today.

Thinking about the text

4 Imagine you could have the four eyewitnesses on a news programme to interview them about their experiences in World War I. Working in a group of five, think of some questions the programme host could ask, and the answers the eyewitnesses would give, which would help your viewers to understand more about the war. Perform your interview for the rest of your class.

5 Discuss the language of the text with a partner. Answer these questions:
   ● How do the different eyewitnesses speak or write?
   ● What can you tell about them from the words they use?
   ● Who seems most formal? Who seems most informal?
   ● Which is the most emotional account? Which is the most impersonal?

Discuss the similarities and differences you notice.

Not My Best Side

Before you read

1   This poem is about the characters in the painting *Saint George and the Dragon*. Look at the painting and write a paragraph giving your first impressions. Use these questions to help you:
   ● What is happening?
   ● What is the backdrop?
   ● Where do you think the scene is supposed to be set?
   ● What do you like or dislike in the scene?
   ● What surprises you about it?
   ● What impression does it give you of the three main characters?

What's it about?

2   Each section of the poem is narrated by a different character in the painting – the dragon, the princess and George. For each character, write down:
   a what impression you get of each character from reading the poem
   b how this impression is different from the view you formed from looking at the picture.

3   Write down some of the things the dragon complains about. Why is he unhappy with:
   a the painter's work
   b the image of George
   c the horse
   d the maiden?

Thinking about the text

4   Do the poem and painting tell us different things about the story of George and the Dragon? Write a paragraph or two describing what you like and dislike in each.

5   Working in a small group, discuss what differences you notice in the language used by the three characters in the poem. Which is most formal, most chatty, most complex? What clues do the words and phrases used by each character give you about what she or he is like?

Compare and contrast

1 The texts in this section all describe different aspects of what life was like in the past.
   a Draw a time-line – a bit like a washing line – and label the texts on it in chronological order. Put the text about the earliest date on the left and the text about the most recent period on the right.
   b Then using a highlighting pen, or coloured crayons, show which texts leave you with a positive view of life at the time and which leave you with a negative impression. You could use bright and dark colours, or smiley and frowning faces.

2 Choose two texts that tell you about ways of life you did not previously know much about. Draw two sketches showing what you have learned from them. Think about:
   - what life was like in the time
   - what people did in their lives
   - how the things people used (tools, technology and household items) were different then.

   Label your drawings to show the main ways in which life was different from now.

3 Choose two or three of the texts and compare the way they are written, using these prompts:
   a Which text uses the simplest language?
   b Which text was the hardest to understand?
   c Which text creates the most vivid picture of life in the past?
   d Which text is most factual?
   e Which text did you most enjoy?

4 Choose the text you enjoyed reading the most. Write a one-paragraph note to the author saying:
   a what you enjoyed about it
   b what you learned from it
   c why you liked it more than the others.

5 Imagine that you are a Martian. You read the texts in this section in order to find out about life on Earth. What impression do you get of British people and Earth? Write a letter to a Martian friend, telling them what you think of Earth and its people.

5 The world about us

This section looks at how we affect the world around us – how we see it, how we shape it, and how we are damaging it. In these texts you will learn about:

- scientific thinkers and discoveries
- the impact our lifestyles are having on the planet
- how we feed ourselves and fail to feed our global neighbours.

Overall, this section reminds us that we face many challenges. But it isn't all bleak. There are also texts to remind us that when we human beings act as global citizens we can create a brighter future.

Activities

1   The world faces a range of problems, including:
    - terrorism
    - global warming
    - an energy crisis
    - the way we treat animals
    - poverty and disease in some developing countries
    - the destruction of nature and the possible extinction of species of plants and animals.

    Think of an issue that you feel particularly strongly about. What can ordinary people – the pupils and staff at your school, for example – do to help? Write a paragraph about the issue, describing what it is and why you feel strongly about it. Then make a list of action points, explaining what people could do in their own lives to make a difference.

2   In the 1950s it was popular to make predictions about what the world would be like at the turn of the century – for example, it was thought that robots would do many of the boring jobs humans had to do. What are your predictions for the next 50 years? In what ways do you think the world will be a better place in 50 years' time? In what ways do you think it will be worse? Write down three positive and two negative predictions.

3   This section is based upon some of the big issues facing the world. Look at the list below and put them in order of most to least important for you personally. Then compare your choices with a friend's.

- recycling waste products
- cutting down travel by car
- cutting debts of developing countries
- reducing world poverty
- using science to grow more crops for people across the world
- reducing animal cruelty
- tackling obesity
- reducing airline travel
- reducing wasteful packaging
- cutting carbon emissions into the atmosphere

The Destructors

by Graham Greene

Graham Greene's shocking story was written in 1954. It is shocking because it shows how a group of children systematically destroy an old man's home – just for fun.

People sometimes talk negatively about young people of today, criticising the way they behave, how they dress, their attitudes and values. This is nothing new. Young people have often been a target for criticism from adults. Even back in 1274, Peter the Hermit said: 'Young people today think of nothing but themselves. They have no reverence for parents or old age.'

Graham Greene's story was written more than half a century ago, showing us that vandalism and destruction are not new.

1

It was on the eve of August Bank Holiday that the latest recruit became the leader of the Wormsley Common Gang. No one was surprised except Mike, but Mike at the age of nine was surprised by everything. 'If you don't shut your mouth,' somebody once said to him, 'you'll get a frog down it.' After that Mike kept his teeth tightly clamped except when the surprise was too great.

The new recruit had been with the gang since the begin-ning of the summer holidays, and there were possibilities about his brooding silence that all recognised. He never wasted a word even to tell his name until that was required of him by the rules. When he said 'Trevor' it was a statement of fact, not as it would have been with the others a statement of shame or defiance. Nor did anyone laugh except Mike, who finding himself without support and meeting the dark gaze of the newcomer opened his mouth and was quiet again. There was every reason why T, as he was afterwards referred to, should have been an object of mockery – there was his name (and they substituted the initial because otherwise they had no excuse not to laugh at it), the fact that his father, a former architect and present clerk,[1] had 'come down in the world' and that his mother considered herself better than the neighbours. What but an odd quality of danger, of the unpredictable, established him in the gang without any ignoble ceremony of initiation?

The gang met every morning in an impromptu car-park, the site of the last bomb of the first blitz.[2] The leader, who was known as Blackie, claimed to have heard it fall, and no one was precise enough in his dates to point out that he would have been one year old and fast asleep on the down platform of Wormsley Common Underground Station. On one side of the car-park leant the first occupied house, No. 3, of the shattered Northwood Terrace – literally leant, for it had suffered from the blast of the bomb and the side walls were supported on wooden struts. A smaller bomb and incendiaries had fallen beyond, so that the house stuck up like a jagged tooth and carried on the further wall relics of its neighbour, a dado,[3] the remains of a fireplace. T, whose words were almost confined to voting 'Yes' or 'No' to the plan of operations proposed each day by Blackie, once startled the whole gang by saying broodingly, 'Wren built that house, Father says.'

'Who's Wren?'

'The man who built St Paul's.'

'Who cares?' Blackie said. 'It's only Old Misery's.'

Old Misery – whose real name was Thomas – had once been a builder and decorator. He lived alone in the crippled house, doing for himself: once a week you could see him coming back across the common with bread and vegetables, and once as the boys played in the car-park he put his head over the smashed wall of his garden and looked at them.

'Been to the lav,' one of the boys said, for it was common knowledge that since the bombs fell something had gone wrong with the pipes of the house and Old Misery was too

---

[1]**clerk**   someone who does administration work in an office

[2]**blitz**   the German air-raids on Britain in 1940

[3]**dado**   short for 'dado rail', the decorative moulding round the lower part of an interior wall

mean to spend money on the property. He could do the redec-
orating himself at cost price, but he had never learnt plumbing.
The lav was a wooden shed at the bottom of the narrow garden
with a star-shaped hole in the door: it had escaped the blast
which had smashed the house next door and sucked out the
window-frames of No. 3.

The next time the gang became aware of Mr Thomas was
more surprising. Blackie, Mike and a thin yellow boy, who for some
reason was called by his surname Summers, met him on the common coming back from the market. Mr Thomas stopped them. He
said glumly, 'You belong to the lot that play in the car-park?'

Mike was about to answer when Blackie stopped him. As
the leader he had responsibilities. 'Suppose we are?' he said
ambiguously.

'I got some chocolates,' Mr Thomas said. 'Don't like 'em
myself. Here you are. Not enough to go round, I don't suppose.
There never is,' he added with sombre conviction. He handed
over three packets of Smarties.

The gang was puzzled and perturbed by this action and
tried to explain it away. 'Bet someone dropped them and he
picked 'em up,' somebody suggested.

'Pinched 'em and then got in a bleeding funk,' another
thought aloud.

'It's a bribe,' Summers said. 'He wants us to stop bouncing
balls on his wall.'

'We'll show him we don't take bribes,' Blackie said, and
they sacrificed the whole morning to the game of bouncing
that only Mike was young enough to enjoy. There was no sign
from Mr Thomas.

Next day T astonished them all. He was late at the ren-
dezvous, and the voting for that day's exploit took place without him. At Blackie's suggestion the gang was to disperse in
pairs, take buses at random and see how many free rides could
be snatched from unwary conductors (the operation was to be
carried out in pairs to avoid cheating). They were drawing lots
for their companions when T arrived.

'Where you been, T?' Blackie asked. 'You can't vote now. You know the rules.'

'I've been there,' T said. He looked at the ground, as though he had thoughts to hide.

'Where?'

'At Old Misery's.' Mike's mouth opened and then hurriedly closed again with a click. He had remembered the frog.

'At Old Misery's?' Blackie said. There was nothing in the rules against it, but he had a sensation that T was treading on dangerous ground. He asked hopefully, 'Did you break in?'

'No. I rang the bell.'

'And what did you say?'

'I said I wanted to see his house.'

'What did he do?'

'He showed it me.'

'Pinch anything?'

'No.'

'What did you do it for then?'

The gang had gathered round: it was as though an impromptu court were about to form and try some case of deviation. T said, 'It's a beautiful house,' and still watching the ground, meeting no one's eyes, he licked his lips first one way, then the other.

'What do you mean, a beautiful house?' Blackie asked with scorn.

'It's got a staircase two hundred years old like a corkscrew. Nothing holds it up.'

'What do you mean, nothing holds it up. Does it float?'

'It's to do with opposite forces, Old Misery said.'

'What else?'

'There's panelling.'

'Like in the Blue Boar?'

'Two hundred years old.'

'Is Old Misery two hundred years old?'

Mike laughed suddenly and then was quiet again. The meeting was in a serious mood. For the first time since T had strolled into the car-park on the first day of the holidays his position was in danger. It only needed a single use of his real name and the gang would be at his heels.

'What did you do it for?' Blackie asked. He was just, he had no jealousy, he was anxious to retain T in the gang if he could. It was the word 'beautiful' that worried him – that belonged to a class world that you could still see parodied at the Wormsley Common Empire by a man wearing a top hat and a monocle, with a haw-haw accent. He was tempted to say, 'My dear Trevor, old chap,' and unleash his hell hounds. 'If you'd broken in,' he said sadly – that indeed would have been an exploit worthy of the gang.

'This was better,' T said. 'I found out things.' He continued to stare at his feet, not meeting anybody's eye, as though he were absorbed in some dream he was unwilling – or ashamed to share.

'What things?'

'Old Misery's going to be away all tomorrow and Bank Holiday.'

Blackie said with relief, 'You mean we could break in?'

'And pinch things?' somebody asked.

Blackie said, 'Nobody's going to pinch things. Breaking in, that's good enough, isn't it? We don't want any court stuff.'

'I don't want to pinch anything,' T said. 'I've got a better idea.'

'What is it?'

T raised his eyes, as grey and disturbed as the drab August day. 'We'll pull it down,' he said. 'We'll destroy it.'

Blackie gave a single hoot of laughter and then, like Mike, fell quiet, daunted by the serious implacable gaze. 'What'd the police be doing all the time?' he said.

'They'd never know. We'd do it from inside. I've found a way in.' He said with a sort of intensity, 'We'd be like worms, don't you see, in an apple. When we came out again there'd be nothing there, no staircase, no panels, nothing but just walls, and then we'd make the walls fall down – somehow.'

'We'd go to jug,' Blackie said.

'Who's to prove? and anyway we wouldn't have pinched anything.' He added without the smallest flicker of glee, 'There wouldn't be anything to pinch after we'd finished.'

'I've never heard of going to prison for breaking things,' Summers said.

'There wouldn't be time,' Blackie said. 'I've seen house-breakers at work.'

'There are twelve of us,' T said. 'We'd organise.'

'None of us know how . . .'

'I know,' T said. He looked across at Blackie. 'Have you got a better plan?'

'Today,' Mike said tactlessly, 'we're pinching free rides . . .'

'Free rides,' T said. 'Kid stuff. You can stand down, Blackie, if you'd rather . . .'

'The gang's got to vote.'

'Put it up then.'

Blackie said uneasily, 'It's proposed that tomorrow and Monday we destroy Old Misery's house.'

'Here, here,' said a fat boy called Joe. 'Who's in favour?'

T said, 'It's carried.'

'How do we start?' Summers asked.

'He'll tell you,' Blackie said. It was the end of his leadership. He went away to the back of the car-park and began to kick a stone, dribbling it this way and that. There was only one old Morris in the park, for few cars were left there except lorries: without an attendant there was no safety. He took a flying kick at the car and scraped a little paint off the rear mudguard. Beyond, paying no more attention to him than to a stranger, the gang had gathered round T; Blackie was dimly aware of the fickleness of favour. He thought of going home, of never returning, of letting them all discover the hollowness of T's leadership, but suppose after all what T proposed was possible, nothing like it had ever been done before. The fame of the Wormsley Common car-park gang would surely reach around London. There would be headlines in the papers. Even the grown-up gangs who ran the betting at the all-in wrestling and the barrow-boys would hear with respect of how Old Misery's house had been destroyed. Driven by the pure, simple and altruistic ambition of fame for the gang,

Blackie came back to where T stood in the shadow of Old Misery's wall.

T was giving his orders with decision: it was as though this plan had been with him all his life, pondered through the seasons, now in his fifteenth year crystallised with the pain of puberty. 'You,' he said to Mike, 'bring some big nails, the biggest you can find, and a hammer. Anybody who can, better bring a hammer and a screwdriver. We'll need plenty of them. Chisels too. We can't have too many chisels. Can anybody bring a saw?'

'I can,' Mike said.

'Not a child's saw,' T said. 'A real saw.'

Blackie realised he had raised his hand like any ordinary member of the gang.

'Right, you bring one, Blackie. But now there's a difficulty. We want a hacksaw.'

'What's a hacksaw?' someone asked.

'You can get 'em at Woolworth's,' Summers said.

The fat boy called Joe said gloomily, 'I knew it would end in a collection.'

'I'll get one myself,' T said. 'I don't want your money. But I can't buy a sledge-hammer.'

Blackie said, 'They are working on No. 15. I know where they'll leave their stuff for Bank Holiday.'

'Then that's all,' T said. 'We meet here at nine sharp.'

'I've got to go to church,' Mike said.

'Come over the wall and whistle. We'll let you in.'

2

On Sunday morning all were punctual except Blackie, even Mike. Mike had a stroke of luck. His mother felt ill, his father was tired after Saturday night, and he was told to go to church alone with many warnings of what would happen if he strayed. Blackie had difficulty in smuggling out the saw, and then in finding the sledge-hammer at the back of No. 15. He approached the house from a lane at the rear of the garden, for fear of the policeman's beat along the main road. The tired evergreens kept off a stormy sun: another wet Bank Holiday was being prepared over the Atlantic, beginning in swirls of dust under the trees. Blackie climbed the wall into Misery's garden.

There was no sign of anybody anywhere. The lav stood like a tomb in a neglected graveyard. The curtains were drawn. The house slept. Blackie lumbered nearer with the saw and the sledge-hammer. Perhaps after all nobody had turned up: the plan had been a wild invention: they had woken wiser. But when he came close to the back door he could hear a confusion of sound hardly louder than a hive in swarm: a clickety-clack, a bang bang, a scraping, a creaking, a sudden painful crack. He thought: it's true; and whistled.

They opened the back door to him and he came in. He had at once the impression of organisation, very different from the old happy-go-lucky ways under his leadership. For a while he wandered up and down stairs looking for T. Nobody addressed him: he had a sense of great urgency, and already he could begin to see the plan. The interior of the house was being carefully demolished without touching the walls. Summers with hammer and chisel was ripping out the skirting-boards in the ground floor dining-room: he had already smashed the panels of the door. In the same room Joe was heaving up the parquet blocks, exposing the soft wood floorboards over the cellar. Coils of wire came out of the damaged skirting; and Mike sat happily on the floor clipping the wires.

On the curved stairs two of the gang were working hard with an inadequate child's saw on the banisters – when they saw Blackie's big saw they signalled for it wordlessly. When he next saw them a quarter of the banisters had been dropped into the hall. He found T at last in the bathroom – he sat moodily in the least cared-for room in the house, listening to the sounds coming up from below.

'You've really done it,' Blackie said with awe. 'What's going to happen?'

'We've only just begun,' T said. He looked at the sledge-hammer and gave his instructions. 'You stay here and break the bath and the wash-basin. Don't bother about the pipes. They come later.'

Mike appeared at the door. 'I've finished the wires, T,' he said.

'Good. You've just got to go wandering round now. The kitchen's in the basement. Smash all the china and glass and bottles you can lay hold of. Don't turn on the taps – we don't want a flood – yet. Then go into all the rooms and turn out the drawers. If they are locked get one of the others to break them open. Tear up any papers you find and smash all the ornaments. Better take a carving knife with you from the kitchen. The bedroom's opposite here. Open the pillows and tear up the sheets. That's enough for the moment. And you, Blackie, when you've finished in here crack the plaster in the passage up with your sledge-hammer.'

'What are you going to do?' Blackie asked.

'I'm looking for something special,' T said.

It was nearly lunch-time before Blackie had finished and went in search of T. Chaos had advanced. The kitchen was a shambles of broken glass and china. The dining-room was stripped of parquet, the skirting was up, the door had been taken off its hinges, and the destroyers had moved up a floor. Streaks of light came in through the closed shutters where they worked with the seriousness of creators – and destruction after all is a form of creation. A kind of imagination had seen this house as it had now become.

Mike said, 'I've got to go home for dinner.'

'Who else?' T asked, but all the others on one excuse or another had brought provisions with them.

They squatted in the ruins of the room and swapped unwanted sandwiches. Half an hour for lunch and they were at work again. By the time Mike returned they were on the top floor, and by six the superficial damage was completed. The doors were all off, all the skirtings raised, the furniture pillaged and ripped and smashed – no one could have slept in the house except on a bed of broken plaster. T gave his orders – eight o'clock next morning, and to escape notice they climbed singly over the garden wall; into the car-park. Only Blackie and T were left: the light had nearly gone, and when they touched a switch, nothing worked – Mike had done his job thoroughly.

'Did you find anything special?' Blackie asked.

T nodded. 'Come over here,' he said, 'and look.' Out of both pockets he drew bundles of pound notes. 'Old Misery's savings,' he said. 'Mike ripped out the mattress, but he missed them.'

'What are you going to do? Share them?'

'We aren't thieves,' T said. 'Nobody's going to steal anything from this house. I kept these for you and me – a celebration.' He knelt down on the floor and counted them out – there were seventy in all. 'We'll burn them,' he said, 'one by one,' and taking it in turns they held a note upwards and lit the top corner, so that the flame burnt slowly towards their fingers. The grey ash floated above them and fell on their heads like age. 'I'd like to see Old Misery's face when we are through,' T said.

'You hate him a lot?' Blackie asked.

'Of course I don't hate him,' T said. 'There'd be no fun if I hated him.' The last burning note illuminated his brooding face. 'All this hate and love,' he said, 'it's soft, it's hooey. There's only things, Blackie,' and he looked round the room crowded with the unfamiliar shadows of half things, broken things, former things. 'I'll race you home, Blackie,' he said.

3

Next morning the serious destruction started. Two were missing – Mike and another boy whose parents were off to Southend and Brighton in spite of the slow warm drops that had begun to fall and the rumble of thunder in the estuary like the first guns of the old blitz. 'We've got to hurry,' T said.

Summers was restive. 'Haven't we done enough?' he asked. 'I've been given a bob for slot machines. This is like work.'

'We've hardly started,' T said. 'Why, there's all the floors left, and the stairs. We haven't taken out a single window. You voted like the others. We are going to destroy this house. There won't be anything left when we've finished.'

They began again on the first floor picking up the top floor-boards next to the outer wall, leaving the joists exposed. Then they sawed through the joists and retreated into the hall, as what was left of the floor heeled and sank. They had learnt with prac-tice, and the second floor collapsed more easily. By the evening an odd exhilaration seized them as they looked down the great hollow of the house. They ran risks and made mistakes: when they thought of the windows it was too late to reach them. 'Cor,' Joe said, and dropped a penny down into the dry rubble-filled well. It cracked and span amongst the broken glass.

'Why did we start this?' Summers asked with astonish-ment; T was already on the ground, digging at the rubble, clear-ing a space along the outer wall.

'Turn on the taps,' he said. 'It's too dark for anyone to see now, and in the morning it won't matter.' The water overtook them on the stairs and fell through the floorless rooms.

It was then they heard Mike's whistle at the back. 'Something's wrong,' Blackie said. They could hear his urgent breathing as they unlocked the door.

'The bogies?' Summers asked.

'Old Misery,' Mike said. 'He's on his way,' he said with pride.

'But why?' T said. 'He told me . . . ' He protested with the fury of the child he had never been, 'It isn't fair.'

'He was down at Southend,' Mike said, 'and he was on the train coming back. Said it was too cold and wet.' He paused and gazed at the water. 'My, you've had a storm here. Is the roof leaking?'

'How long will he be?'

'Five minutes. I gave Ma the slip and ran.'

'We'd better clear,' Summers said. 'We've done enough, anyway.'

'Oh no, we haven't. Anybody could do this.' 'This' was the shattered hollowed house with nothing left but the walls. Yet walls could be preserved. Façades were valuable. They could build inside again more beautifully than before. This could again be a home. He said angrily, 'We've got to finish. Don't move. Let me think.'

'There's no time,' a boy said.

'There's got to be a way,' T said. 'We couldn't have got this far . . .'

'We've done a lot,' Blackie said.

'No. No, we haven't. Somebody watch the front.'

'We can't do any more.'

'He may come in at the back.'

'Watch the back too.' T began to plead. 'Just give me a minute and I'll fix it. I swear I'll fix it.' But his authority had gone with his ambiguity. He was only one of the gang. 'Please,' he said.

'Please,' Summers mimicked him, and then suddenly struck home with the fatal name. 'Run along home, Trevor.'

T stood with his back to the rubble like a boxer knocked groggy against the ropes. He had no words as his dreams shook and slid. Then Blackie acted before the gang had time to laugh, pushing Summers backward. 'I'll watch the front, T,' he said, and cautiously he opened the shutters of the hall. The grey wet common stretched ahead, and the lamps gleamed in the puddles. 'Someone's coming, T. No, it's not him. What's your plan, T?'

'Tell Mike to go out to the lav and hide close beside it. When he hears me whistle he's got to count ten and start to shout.'

'Shout what?'

'Oh, "Help", anything.'

'You hear, Mike?' Blackie said. He was the leader again. He took a quick look between the shutters. 'He's coming, T.'

'Quick, Mike. The lav. Stay here, Blackie, all of you; till I yell.'

'Where are you going, T?'

'Don't worry. I'll see to this. I said I would, didn't I?'

Old Misery came limping off the common. He had mud on his shoes and he stopped to scrape them on the pavement's edge. He didn't want to soil his house, which stood jagged and dark between the bomb-sites, saved so narrowly, as he believed, from destruction. Even the fan-light had been left unbroken by the bomb's blast. Somewhere somebody whistled. Old Misery looked sharply round. He didn't trust whistles. A child was shouting: it seemed to come from his own garden. Then a boy ran into the road from the car-park. 'Mr Thomas,' he called, 'Mr Thomas.'

'What is it?'

'I'm terribly sorry, Mr Thomas. One of us got taken short, and we thought you wouldn't mind, and now he can't get out.'

'What do you mean, boy?'

'He's got stuck in your lav.'

'He'd no business . . . Haven't I seen you before?'

'You showed me your house.'

'So I did. So I did. That doesn't give you the right to . . . '

'Do hurry, Mr Thomas. He'll suffocate.'

'Nonsense. He can't suffocate. Wait till I put my bag in.'

'I'll carry your bag.'

'Oh no, you don't. I carry my own.'

'This way, Mr Thomas.'

'I can't get in the garden that way. I've got to go through the house.'

'But you can get in the garden this way, Mr Thomas. We often do.'

'You often do?' He followed the boy with a scandalised fascination. 'When? What right . . . ?'

'Do you see . . . ? The wall's low.'

'I'm not going to climb walls into my own garden. It's absurd.'

'This is how we do it. One foot here, one foot there, and over.' The boy's face peered down, an arm shot out and Mr Thomas found his bag taken and deposited on the other side of the wall.

'Give me back my bag,' Mr Thomas said. From the loo a boy yelled and yelled. 'I'll call the police.'

'Your bag's all right, Mr Thomas. Look. One foot there. On your right. Now just above. To your left.' Mr Thomas climbed over his own garden wall. 'Here's your bag, Mr Thomas.'

'I'll have the wall built up,' Mr Thomas said, 'I'll not have you boys coming over here, using my loo.' He stumbled on the path, but the boy caught his elbow and supported him. 'Thank you, thank you, my boy,' he murmured automatically. Somebody shouted again through the dark. 'I'm coming, I'm coming,' Mr Thomas called. He said to the boy beside him, 'I'm not unreasonable. Been a boy myself. As long as things are done regular. I don't mind you playing round the place Saturday mornings. Sometimes I like company. Only it's got to be regular. One of you asks leave and I say Yes. Sometimes I'll say No. Won't feel like it. And you come in at the front door and out at the back. No garden walls.'

'Do get him out, Mr Thomas.'

'He won't come to any harm in my loo,' Mr Thomas said, stumbling slowly down the garden. 'Oh, my rheumatics,' he said. 'Always get 'em on Bank Holiday. I've got to be careful. There's loose stones here. Give me your hand. Do you know what my horoscope said yesterday? "Abstain from any dealings in first half of week. Danger of serious crash." That might be on this path,' Mr Thomas said. 'They speak in parables and double meanings.' He paused at the door of the loo. 'What's the matter in there?' he called. There was no reply.

'Perhaps he's fainted,' the boy said.

'Not in my loo. Here, you, come out,' Mr Thomas said, and giving a great jerk at the door he nearly fell on his back when it swung easily open. A hand first supported him and then pushed him hard. His head hit the opposite wall and he sat heavily down. His bag hit his feet. A hand whipped the key out of the lock and the door slammed. 'Let me out,' he called, and heard the key turn in the lock. 'A serious crash,' he thought, and felt dithery and confused and old.

A voice spoke to him softly through the star-shaped hole in the door. 'Don't worry, Mr Thomas,' it said, 'we won't hurt you, not if you stay quiet.'

Mr Thomas put his head between his hands and pondered. He had noticed that there was only one lorry in the car-park, and he felt certain that the driver would not come for it before the morning. Nobody could hear him from the road in front and the lane at the back was seldom used. Anyone who passed there would be hurrying home and would not pause for what they would certainly take to be drunken cries. And if he did call 'Help', who, on a lonely Bank Holiday evening, would have the courage to investigate? Mr Thomas sat on the loo and pondered with the wisdom of age.

After a while it seemed to him that there were sounds in the silence – they were faint and came from the direction of his house. He stood up and peered through the ventilation-hole – between the cracks in one of the shutters he saw a light, not the light of a lamp, but the wavering light that a candle might give. Then he thought he heard the sound of hammering and scraping and chipping. He thought of burglars – perhaps they had employed the boy as a scout, but why should burglars engage in what sounded more and more like a stealthy form of carpentry? Mr Thomas let out an experimental yell, but nobody answered. The noise could not even have reached his enemies.

4

Mike had gone home to bed, but the rest stayed. The question of leadership no longer concerned the gang. With nails, chisels, screwdrivers, anything that was sharp and penetrating, they moved around the inner walls worrying at the mortar between the bricks. They started too high, and it was Blackie who hit on the damp course and realised the work could be halved if they weakened the joints immediately above. It was a long, tiring, unamusing job, but at last it was finished. The gutted house stood there balanced on a few inches of mortar between the damp course and the bricks.

There remained the most dangerous task of all, out in the open at the edge of the bomb-site. Summers was sent to watch the road for passers-by, and Mr Thomas, sitting on the loo, heard clearly now the sound of sawing. It no longer came from the house, and that a little reassured him. He felt less concerned. Perhaps the other noises too had no significance.

A voice spoke to him through the hole. 'Mr Thomas.'

'Let me out,' Mr Thomas said sternly.

'Here's a blanket,' the voice said, and a long grey sausage was worked through the hole and fell in swathes over Mr Thomas's head.

'There's nothing personal,' the voice said. 'We want you to be comfortable tonight.'

'Tonight,' Mr Thomas repeated incredulously.

'Catch,' the voice said. 'Penny buns – we've buttered them, and sausage-rolls. We don't want you to starve, Mr Thomas.'

Mr Thomas pleaded desperately. 'A joke's a joke, boy. Let me out and I won't say a thing. I've got rheumatics. I got to sleep comfortable.'

'You wouldn't be comfortable, not in your house, you wouldn't. Not now.'

'What do you mean, boy?' But the footsteps receded. There was only the silence of night: no sound of sawing. Mr Thomas tried one more yell, but he was daunted and rebuked by the silence – a long way off an owl hooted and made away again on its muffled flight through the soundless world.

At seven next morning the driver came to fetch his lorry. He climbed into the seat and tried to start the engine. He was vaguely aware of a voice shouting, but it didn't concern him. At last the engine responded and he backed the lorry until it touched the great wooden shore that supported Mr Thomas's house. That way he could drive right out and down the street without reversing. The lorry moved forward, was momentarily checked as though something were pulling it from behind, and then went on to the sound of a long rumbling crash. The driver was astonished to see bricks bouncing ahead of him, while stones hit the roof of his cab. He put on his brakes. When he climbed out the whole landscape had suddenly altered. There was no house beside the car-park, only a hill of rubble. He went round and examined the back of his lorry for damage, and found a rope tied there that was still twisted at the other end round part of a wooden strut.

The driver again became aware of somebody shouting. It came from the wooden erection which was the nearest thing to a house in that desolation of broken brick. The driver climbed the smashed wall and unlocked the door. Mr Thomas came out of the loo. He was wearing a grey blanket to which flakes of pastry adhered. He gave a sobbing cry. 'My house,' he said. 'Where's my house?'

'Search me,' the driver said. His eye lit on the remains of a bath and what had once been a dresser and he began to laugh. There wasn't anything left anywhere.

'How dare you laugh,' Mr Thomas said. 'It was my house. My house.'

'I'm sorry,' the driver said, making heroic efforts, but when he remembered the sudden check of his lorry, the crash of bricks falling, he became convulsed again. One moment the house had stood there with such dignity between the bomb-sites like a man in a top hat, and then, bang, crash, there wasn't anything left – not anything. He said, 'I'm sorry. I can't help it, Mr Thomas. There's nothing personal, but you got to admit it's funny.'

Further reading

Graham Greene's powerful and often disturbing tales can be found in his *Complete Short Stories* (Penguin Books Ltd, 2005). Another disturbing account of the effect of peer pressure leading to terrible violence is William Golding's *Lord of the Flies* (Faber and Faber, 1997).

We Are Going to See the Rabbit
by Alan Brownjohn

Alan Brownjohn was a teacher and poet. This poem is actually called *After Prévert* (Prévert was a French poet and film screenwriter), but is better known as *We Are Going to See the Rabbit*. It is a poem about a strange future world.

We are going to see the rabbit,
We are going to see the rabbit.
Which rabbit, people say?
Which rabbit, ask the children?
Which rabbit?
The only rabbit,
The only rabbit in England,
Sitting behind a barbed-wire fence
Under the floodlights, neon lights,
Sodium[1] lights,
Nibbling grass
On the only patch of grass
In England, in England
(Except the grass by the hoardings
Which doesn't count.)
We are going to see the rabbit
And we must be there on time.

First we shall go by escalator,
Then we shall go by underground,
And then we shall go by motorway
And then by helicopterway,
And the last ten yards we shall have to go
On foot.

---

[1]**sodium**   a chemical element that burns with a bright yellow flame

And now we are going
All the way to see the rabbit,
We are nearly there,
We are longing to see it,
And so is the crowd
Which is here in thousands
With mounted policemen
And big loudspeakers
And bands and banners,
And everyone has come a long way.
But soon we shall see it
Sitting and nibbling
The blades of grass
On the only patch of grass
In – but something has gone wrong!
Why is everyone so angry,
Why is everyone jostling
And slanging and complaining?

The rabbit has gone,
Yes, the rabbit has gone.
He has actually burrowed down into the earth
And made himself a warren, under the earth,
Despite all these people.
And what shall we do?
What *can* we do?
It is all a pity, you must be disappointed,
Go home and do something else for today,
Go home again, go home for today.
For you cannot hear the rabbit, under the earth,
Remarking rather sadly to himself, by himself,
As he rests in his warren, under the earth:
'It won't be long, they are bound to come,
They are bound to come and find me, even here.'

Further reading

If you liked this poem, try some of Alan Brownjohn's other poems in *Collected Poems* (Enitharmon Press, 2006). If you'd like to read some more accounts of what the world might be like in the future, see *The Penguin World Omnibus of Science Fiction* (edited by Brian W. Aldiss and Sam J. Lundwall; Penguin Books Ltd, 1986).

Song of the Battery Hen

by Edwin Brock

Edwin Brock (1927–1977) was a British poet who was probably best known for his war poetry. However, he also wrote hard-hitting poems about social issues, such as *Five Ways to Kill a Man* and this one, *Song of the Battery Hen*, which tells readers about conditions on a factory farm through the eyes of a hen.

We can't grumble about accommodation:
we have a new concrete floor that's
always dry, four walls that are
painted white, and a sheet-iron roof
the rain drums on. A fan blows warm air
beneath our feet to disperse[1] the smell
of chicken-shit and, on dull days,
fluorescent lighting sees us.

---

[1]**disperse**   spread out

You can tell me: if you come by
the North door, I am in the twelfth pen
on the left-hand side of the third row
from the floor; and in that pen
I am usually the middle one of three.
But, even without directions, you'd
discover me. I have the same orange-
red comb, yellow beak and auburn
feathers, but as the door opens and you
hear above the electric fan a kind of
one-word wail, I am the one
who sounds loudest in my head.

Listen. Outside this house there's an
orchard with small moss-green apple
trees; beyond that, two fields of
cabbages; then, on the far side of
the road, a broiler house. Listen:
one cockerel grows out of there, as
tall and proud as the first hour of sun.
Sometimes I stop calling with the others
to listen, and wonder if he hears me.

The next time you come here, look for me.
Notice the way I sound inside my head.
God made us all quite differently,
and blessed us with this expensive home.

Further reading

If you enjoyed this poem, try some more of Edwin Brock's funny and
disturbing poems, which are collected in *Five Ways to Kill a Man: New and
Selected Poems* (Enitharmon Press, 1997). If you want to find out more
about the treatment of animals, a very balanced and informed view is
given on the RSPCA's website: www.rspca.org.uk/

Alexander Graham Bell and the Telephone

by Adam Hart-Davis and Paul Bader

In the past 200 or so years, science and technology have transformed our lives. Even 20 years ago few people would have believed that an entire music, photograph and video library could be carried in a tiny portable box, or that mobile phones would be so small, so easily available, and so powerful.

This essay describes the life of Alexander Graham Bell, the 19th-century inventor of the telephone.

Alexander Graham Bell was born at 16 South Charlotte Street, on the corner of Charlotte Square, in Edinburgh, on 3 March 1847. His father and his grandfather were both authorities on elocution, and it wasn't long before the young Alexander was teaching people how to speak. He was enormously inventive, and not only made the first iron lung, but also bred special sheep with multiple nipples because he thought they would

have more lambs. However, what makes him a legendary inventor is the telephone.

In 1863, at the age of sixteen, Alexander and his brother Melville began some serious research into how speech worked. They started with the anatomy[1] of the mouth and throat and even examined the family cat (after it had died) so they could study the vocal cords in more detail. Studying the pitch of the vowel sounds, they imagined the throat and the mouth like two different-sized bottles. Each makes a different pitch, and they realised that the vowel sounds were a combination of two pitches. Their father, Melville senior, had spent years classifying vocal sounds and came up with a shorthand system called *Visible Speech*, where every sound was represented by a symbol. The idea was to teach the deaf to speak by putting all these sounds together.

They eventually made an elaborate speaking machine to test their theories. Later in 1863, Alexander went to Elgin near the Moray Firth in the north of Scotland to teach elocution at the Weston House Academy, and there, in what is now a Comet store, he first conceived the idea of transmitting speech with electricity.

When Alexander's two brothers died in 1870, the family moved to North America. Alexander settled in Boston, the scientific and academic centre of America, and was soon using *Visible Speech* to teach the deaf. The idea of transmitting speech along a wire never left him, and though he knew little about electricity he knew a good deal about speech and sound. His years of research led him up a few blind alleys, but by 1875 he had come up with a simple receiver that could turn electricity into sound: in other words, a speaker. It was essentially a magnet glued to a diaphragm,[2] and able to move within a coil of wire, so that a change of electric current in the coil would cause the magnet, and therefore also the diaphragm, to move in or out. Thus a varying electrical signal produced a varying sound wave from the speaker.

---

[1]**anatomy**   inner structure (of a part of the body)
[2]**diaphragm**   thin sheet of material that carries vibrations

But he still needed a transmitter. He had no effective way of converting the sounds of the voice into an electric signal. What he needed, as his assistant Tom Watson put it, was to 'generate voice-shaped electric undulations'. He tried a few weird contraptions, including a diaphragm connected to a needle. As he spoke into it, the needle dipped in and out of a bowl of acid. The varying resistance produced a varying electric current from a battery. The great breakthrough came quite by accident on 2 June 1875. Bell and Watson were testing a circuit with one transmitter and two receivers in separate rooms, when Bell switched off the transmitter. Then he heard a note coming from the receiver in his room. Puzzled by this, he went through, and found Watson adjusting the other receiver. Bell realised that, with the transmitter turned off, the note must be coming from the other receiver acting as a transmitter – in other words, as a microphone. At that moment, the telephone was born.

By a fluke, Bell had discovered that the receiver could also work in reverse – instead of making sound when he sent electricity through it, it made electricity when he supplied sound, because the sound moved the diaphragm, the diaphragm moved the magnet in the coil and this generated electricity. Six months went by before he was able to send intelligible speech down the wire, and according to popular legend, and Bell's diary, the first words ever spoken on the telephone were, 'Mr Watson, come here; I want to see you.' Rather peremptory,[3] but no doubt the great man was excited, and no doubt Mr Watson jumped to it with alacrity.

Bell developed his system – he certainly needed a much better microphone – and submitted his patent[4] on St Valentine's Day 1876, just two hours before Elisha Gray, his main rival. The patent was granted on 7 March, and was one of the most valuable patents ever issued. Over 600 lawsuits followed before a Supreme Court decision ruled in Bell's favour in 1893. Meanwhile, Bell

---

[3]**peremptory**   bossy
[4]**patent**   application for the exclusive right to use a design

had made the telephone available to the public in 1877, when the Bell Telephone Company was created. Developments were swift; within a year the first telephone exchange was built in Connecticut and within ten years more than 150,000 people had telephones in the United States alone. Bell married Mabel, the deaf daughter of his financial partner, and signed nearly all of his stock over to her, keeping just ten shares for 'sentimental reasons'. Within three years the price of Bell Telephone Company shares soared from fifty dollars to over a thousand dollars. Alexander was finally a man of independent means.

Bell eventually built a large house in remote Nova Scotia, where the landscape and weather reminded him of Scotland. Here he continued his work with the deaf, including the young Helen Keller.[5] He invented weird aircraft with wings based on triangles; he built a resuscitation device, the forerunner to the iron lung; and experimented with sheep. He had a peculiar notion that sheep with extra nipples would give birth to two or more lambs, and be more productive for farmers. He built Sheepville, a huge village of sheep pens, and spent years counting sheep nipples. The work continued for decades before the US state department announced that there was no link between extra nipples and extra lambs.

Alexander Graham Bell was kind and generous and gave much of his money and time to improving the lives of those around him. He died in 1922 and will be revered for his work with the deaf and celebrated for his invention of the telephone.

Further reading

Adam Hart-Davis and Paul Bader's *100 Local Heroes* (Sutton Publishing, 2000) is full of accounts of famous inventors and engineers. You might also like to try *The Faber Book of Science* by John Carey (Faber and Faber, 2005), a magnificent collection of scientific discoveries and inventions throughout history.

---

[5]**Helen Keller**   American author who at the age of 19 months became deaf and blind

Hunger

by Laurence Binyon

> Laurence Binyon (1869–1943) was a poet and scholar. He is best known for his poem *For the Fallen*, which is regularly read aloud to commemorate the people who lost their lives in war. This lesser-known poem looks at the way hunger, like war, can kill.

I come among the peoples like a shadow.
I sit down by each man's side.

None sees me, but they look on one another,
And know that I am there.

My silence is like the silence of the tide
That buries the playground of children;

Like the deepening of frost in the slow night,
When birds are dead in the morning.

Armies trample, invade, destroy,
With guns roaring from earth and air.

I am more terrible than armies,
I am more feared than cannon.

Kings and chancellors[1] give commands;
I give no command to any;

But I am listened to more than kings
And more than passionate orators.

---

[1]**chancellors**   heads of government

I unswear words, and undo deeds.
Naked things know me.

I am first and last to be felt of the living;
I am Hunger.

Further reading

Laurence Binyon is most famous for writing *For the Fallen,* his poem about war. For more powerful writing about war, see *Forgotten Voices of the Great War* by Max Arthur (Ebury Press, 2003), a collection of first-hand accounts by eyewitnesses and survivors.

Fast Food Nation
by Eric Schlosser

This text explores the way we eat in the western world. Eric Schlosser's book makes us think carefully about what we are eating and the artificial ingredients we are adding. In particular it looks at the artificial flavours that are added to foods to encourage us to buy them.

Since Schlosser's book was published, the government has introduced strict guidelines on what may or may not be sold in schools. See what you think about his section on food additives.

The taste of McDonald's french fries has long been praised by customers, competitors, and even food critics. James Beard loved McDonald's fries. Their distinctive taste does not stem from the type of potatoes that McDonald's buys, the technology that processes them, or the restaurant equipment that fries them. Other chains buy their french fries from the same large processing companies, use Russet Burbanks, and have similar fryers in their restaurant kitchens. The taste of a fast food fry is largely determined by the cooking oil. For decades, McDonald's cooked its french fries in a mixture of about 7 percent cottonseed oil and 93 percent beef tallow.[1] The mix gave the fries their unique flavor – and more saturated beef fat per ounce than a McDonald's hamburger.

Amid a barrage of criticism over the amount of cholesterol[2] in their fries, McDonald's switched to pure vegetable oil in 1990. The switch presented the company with an enormous challenge: how to make fries that subtly taste like beef without cooking them in tallow. A look at the ingredients now used in the preparation of McDonald's french fries suggests how the problem was solved. Toward the end of the list is a seemingly innocuous, yet oddly mysterious phrase: 'natural flavor'. That ingredient helps to explain not only why the fries taste so

---

[1]**tallow**   a fatty substance made from rendered animal fat
[2]**cholesterol**   the fat content in blood cells

good, but also why most fast food – indeed, most of the food Americans eat today – tastes the way it does.

Open your refrigerator, your freezer, your kitchen cupboards, and look at the labels on your food. You'll find 'natural flavor' or 'artificial flavor' in just about every list of ingredients. The similarities between these two broad categories of flavor are far more significant than their differences. Both are man-made additives that give most processed food most of its taste. The initial purchase of a food item may be driven by its packaging or appearance, but subsequent purchases are determined mainly by its taste. About 90 percent of the money that Americans spend on food is used to buy processed food. But the canning, freezing, and dehydrating techniques used to process food destroy most of its flavor. Since the end of World War II, a vast industry has arisen in the United States to make processed food palatable. Without this flavor industry, today's fast food industry could not exist. The names of the leading American fast food chains and the best-selling menu items have become famous worldwide, embedded in our popular culture. Few people, however, can name the companies that manufacture fast food's taste.

The flavor industry is highly secretive. Its leading companies will not divulge the precise formulas of flavor compounds or the identities of clients. The secrecy is deemed essential for protecting the reputation of beloved brands. The fast food chains, understandably, would like the public to believe that the flavors of their food somehow originate in their restaurant kitchens, not in distant factories run by other firms.

The New Jersey Turnpike runs through the heart of the flavor industry, an industrial corridor dotted with refineries and chemical plants. International Flavors & Fragrances (IFF), the world's largest flavor company, has a manufacturing facility off Exit 8A in Dayton, New Jersey; Givaudan, the world's second-largest flavor company, has a plant in East Hanover. Haarmann & Reimer, the largest German flavor company, has a plant in Teterboro, as does Takasago, the largest Japanese flavor company. Flavor Dynamics has a plant in South Plainfield;

Frutarom is in North Bergen; Elan Chemical is in Newark. Dozens of companies manufacture flavors in the corridor between Teaneck and South Brunswick. Indeed, the area produces about two-thirds of the flavor additives sold in the United States.

The IFF plant in Dayton is a huge pale blue building with a modern office complex attached to the front. It sits in an industrial park, not far from a BASF plastics factory, a Jolly French Toast factory, and a plant that manufactures Liz Claiborne cosmetics. Dozens of tractor-trailers were parked at the IFF loading dock the afternoon I visited, and a thin cloud of steam floated from the chimney. Before entering the plant, I signed a nondisclosure form, promising not to reveal the brand names of products that contain IFF flavors. The place reminded me of Willy Wonka's chocolate factory. Wonderful smells drifted through the hallways, men and women in neat white lab coats cheerfully went about their work, and hundreds of little glass bottles sat on laboratory tables and shelves. The bottles contained powerful but fragile flavor chemicals, shielded from light by the brown glass and the round plastic caps shut tight. The long chemical names on the little white labels were as mystifying to me as medieval Latin. They were the odd-sounding names of things that would be mixed and poured and turned into new substances, like magic potions.

I was not invited to see the manufacturing areas of the IFF plant, where it was thought I might discover trade secrets. Instead, I toured various laboratories and pilot kitchens, where the flavors of well-established brands are tested or adjusted, and where whole new flavors are created. IFF's snack and savory lab is responsible for the flavor of potato chips, corn chips, breads, crackers, breakfast cereals, and pet food. The confectionery lab devises the flavor for ice cream, cookies, candies, toothpastes, mouthwashes, and antacids. Everywhere I looked, I saw famous, widely advertised products sitting on laboratory desks and tables. The beverage lab is full of brightly colored liquids in clear bottles. It comes up with the flavor for popular soft drinks, sport drinks, bottled teas, and wine coolers, for all-natural juice drinks, organic soy drinks, beers, and malt liquors. In one pilot kitchen I saw a dapper food technologist, a middle-aged man with an elegant tie beneath his lab coat, carefully preparing a batch of cookies with white frosting and pink-and-white sprinkles. In another pilot kitchen I saw a pizza oven, a grill, a milk-shake machine, and a french fryer identical to those I'd seen behind the counter at countless fast food restaurants.

In addition to being the world's largest flavor company, IFF manufactures the smell of six of the ten best-selling fine perfumes in the United States, including Estée Lauder's Beautiful, Clinique's Happy, Lancôme's Trésor, and Calvin Klein's Eternity. It also makes the smell of household products such as deodorant, dishwashing detergent, bath soap, shampoo, furniture polish, and floor wax. All of these aromas are made through the same basic process: the manipulation of volatile chemicals to create a particular smell. The basic science behind the scent of your shaving cream is the same as that governing the flavor of your TV dinner.

The aroma of a food can be responsible for as much as 90 percent of its flavor. Scientists now believe that human beings acquired the sense of taste as a way to avoid being poisoned. Edible plants generally taste sweet; deadly ones, bitter. Taste is supposed to help us differentiate food that's good for us from food that's not. The taste buds on our tongues can detect the presence of half a dozen or so basic tastes, including: sweet, sour, bitter, salty, astringent, and umami (a taste discovered by Japanese researchers, a rich and full sense of deliciousness triggered by amino acids in foods such as shellfish, mushrooms, potatoes, and seaweed). Taste buds offer a relatively limited means of detection, however, compared to the human olfactory[3] system, which can perceive thousands of different chemical aromas. Indeed 'flavor' is primarily the smell of gases being released by the chemicals you've just put in your mouth.

---

[3]**olfactory**   relating to the sense of smell

The act of drinking, sucking, or chewing a substance releases its volatile gases. They flow out of the mouth and up the nostrils, or up the passageway in the back of the mouth, to a thin layer of nerve cells called the olfactory epithelium, located at the base of the nose, right between the eyes. The brain combines the complex smell signals from the epithelium with the simple taste signals from the tongue, assigns a flavor to what's in your mouth, and decides if it's something you want to eat.

Babies like sweet tastes and reject bitter ones; we know this because scientists have rubbed various flavors inside the mouths of infants and then recorded their facial reactions. A person's food preferences, like his or her personality, are formed during the first few years of life, through a process of socialization. Toddlers can learn to enjoy hot and spicy food, bland health food, or fast food, depending upon what the people around them eat. The human sense of smell is still not fully understood and can be greatly affected by psychological factors and expectations. The mind filters out the overwhelming majority of chemical aromas that surround us, focusing intently on some, ignoring others. People can grow accustomed to bad smells or good smells; they stop noticing what once seemed overpowering. Aroma and memory are somehow inextricably linked. A smell can suddenly evoke a long-forgotten moment. The flavors of childhood foods seem to leave an indelible mark, and adults often return to them, without always knowing why. These 'comfort foods' become a source of pleasure and reassurance, a fact that fast food chains work hard to promote. Childhood memories of Happy Meals can translate into frequent adult visits to McDonald's, like those of the chain's 'heavy users,' the customers who eat there four or five times a week.

The human craving for flavor has been a largely unacknowledged and unexamined force in history. Royal empires have been built, unexplored lands have been traversed, great religions and philosophies have been forever changed by the spice trade. In 1492 Christopher Columbus set sail to find seasoning. Today the influence of flavor in the world market-place is no less decisive. The rise and fall of corporate empires – of soft drink companies, snack food companies, and fast food chains – is frequently determined by how their products taste.

The flavor industry emerged in the mid-nineteenth century, as processed foods began to be manufactured on a large scale. Recognizing the need for flavor additives, the early food processors turned to perfume companies that had years of experience working with essential oils and volatile aromas. The great perfume houses of England, France, and the Netherlands produced many of the first flavor compounds. In the early part of the twentieth century, Germany's powerful chemical industry assumed the technological lead in flavor production. Legend has it that a German scientist discovered methyl anthranilate, one of the first artificial flavors, by accident while mixing chemicals in his laboratory. Suddenly the lab was filled with the sweet smell of grapes. Methyl anthranilate later became the chief flavoring compound of grape Kool-Aid. After World War II, much of the perfume industry shifted from Europe to the United States, settling in New York City near the garment district and the fashion houses. The flavor industry came with it, subsequently moving to New Jersey to gain more plant capacity. Man-made flavor additives were used mainly in baked goods, candies, and sodas until the 1950s, when sales of processed food began to soar. The invention of gas chromatographs and mass spectrometers – machines capable of detecting volatile gases at low levels – vastly increased the number of flavors that could be synthesized. By the mid-1960s the American flavor industry was churning out compounds to supply the taste of Pop Tarts, Bac-Os, Tab, Tang, Filet-O-Fish sandwiches, and literally thousands of other new foods.

The American flavor industry now has annual revenues of about $1.4 billion. Approximately ten thousand new processed food products are introduced every year in the United States. Almost all of them require flavor additives. And about nine out of every ten of these new food products fail. The latest flavor innovations and corporate realignments are heralded in publications such as *Food Chemical News*, *Food Engineering*, *Chemical Market Reporter*, and *Food Product Design*. The growth of IFF has mirrored that of the flavor industry as a whole. IFF was formed in 1958, through the merger of two small companies. Its annual revenues have grown almost fifteenfold since the early 1970s, and it now has manufacturing facilities in twenty countries.

The quality that people seek most of all in a food, its flavor, is usually present in a quantity too infinitesimal to be measured by any traditional culinary terms such as ounces or teaspoons. Today's sophisticated spectrometers, gas chromatographs, and headspace vapor analyzers provide a detailed map of a food's flavor components, detecting chemical aromas in amounts as low as one part per billion. The human nose, however, is still more sensitive than any machine yet invented. A nose can detect aromas present in quantities of a few parts per trillion – an amount equivalent to 0.000,000,000,003 percent. Complex aromas, like those of coffee or roasted meat, may be composed of volatile gases from nearly a thousand different chemicals. The smell of a strawberry arises from the interaction of at least 350 different chemicals that are present in minute amounts. The chemical that provides the dominant flavor of bell pepper can be tasted in amounts as low as .02 parts per billion; one drop is sufficient to add flavor to five average size swimming pools. The flavor additive usually comes last, or second to last, in a processed food's list of ingredients (chemicals that add color are frequently used in even smaller amounts). As a result, the flavor of a processed food often costs less than its packaging. Soft drinks contain a larger proportion of flavor additives than most products. The flavor in a twelve-ounce can of Coke costs about half a cent.

The Food and Drug Administration does not require flavor companies to disclose the ingredients of their additives, so long as all the chemicals are considered by the agency to be GRAS (Generally Regarded As Safe). This lack of public disclosure enables the companies to maintain the secrecy of their formulas. It also hides the fact that flavor compounds sometimes contain more ingredients than the foods being given their taste. The ubiquitous phrase 'artificial strawberry flavor' gives little hint of the chemical wizardry and manufacturing skill that can make a highly processed food taste like a strawberry.

Further reading

To see the effects of fast food when eaten three times a day, watch Morgan Spurlock's fascinating documentary, *Super Size Me*, available on DVD. To learn more about English traditions in cooking, browse through Alan Davidson's *The Oxford Companion to Food* (Oxford University Press, 2006), which is a mouthwatering and fascinating read.

Facts to Change the World

by Jessica Williams

One of the most powerful books published in the past few years is Jessica Williams's *50 Facts that Should Change the World*. It is a collection of articles about our world, and in particular what we are doing to it by ignoring our responsibilities to the developing world.

Every day, one in five of the world's population – some 800 million people – go hungry

At the beginning of the 21st century, when the rich world is enjoying the benefits of scientific and medical research and looking forward to long, prosperous lives, it is difficult to comprehend why so much of the world's population should still go hungry.

The statistics tell of a problem of immense proportions. Eight hundred million go hungry every day. Two billion people suffer from chronic malnutrition. Eighteen million die each year from hunger-related diseases. Two billion people suffer from micro-nutrient deficiencies, which lead to chronic health problems. Around half of the deaths of children under five (10 million each year) are associated with malnutrition. Famines occur where there is an acute and extreme shortage of food for a large number of people, but hunger can persist over many years and its long-term effects can be just as devastating. The World Health Organization (WHO) says that hunger and malnutrition are among the most serious problems facing the world's poor.

And yet, incredibly, this is not caused by food shortages. The world produces enough food each year to feed all of its inhabitants: if it were shared out evenly, everyone would have enough to eat. Nutritionists consider that a healthy diet provides 2,500 calories of energy a day. In the USA, the average person consumes 3,600 calories a day. In Somalia, they get 1,500.

Food production has kept pace with global demand, and prices for staple foods like rice and other cereals have fallen. So why are so many still suffering?

The Nobel-Prize-winning economist Amartya Sen is one of the world's foremost authorities on the causes of hunger. He notes that hunger is caused not by a country's inability to produce food but by a lack of income. Poor people have no money to secure a constant food supply, and no resources to grow their own food.

Professor Sen argues that political circumstances are often to blame. Famines may threaten the existence of a democratic government, but where democracy is absent or compromised, the government will often lack the motivation to tackle the problem. 'Indeed, as a country like Zimbabwe ceases to be a functioning democracy,' Professor Sen writes, 'its earlier ability to avoid famines in very adverse food situations (for which Zimbabwe had an excellent record in the 1970s and 1980s) becomes weakened. A more authoritarian Zimbabwe is now facing considerable danger of famine.'

Armed conflict also places a major strain on food security. The UN Food and Agriculture Organization (FAO) found that of eighteen African countries facing food emergencies in 2001, eight were involved in conflict and a further three were suffering its after-effects. In times of war, a government will divert resources away from food production in favour of the military effort. Food distribution and transport networks are disrupted, and where an area is under dispute it may be too dangerous for subsistence farmers to tend their land. In Rwanda in 1995, war displaced three out of four farmers and cut the harvest in half.

Hunger is also, callously,[1] used as a tool of war. One side may try to starve the other into submission, seizing or destroying food stocks and diverting food aid from the needy to the armed forces. Lands may be mined or water sources polluted. In the aftermath of conflict, it is difficult or impossible for

---

[1]**callously**   cruelly

communities to rebuild their food sources. Armed violence in Southern and Western Africa and Central America has left generations of young people without any farming skills at all – the only reality they knew was conflict, so the only training they have is in the art of fighting.

This disappearance of traditional farming techniques is also happening in areas hit hard by the HIV/Aids crisis. Malnutrition has been linked to an earlier onset of Aids symptoms after HIV infection, and it increases the likelihood of opportunistic infection – thus further shortening the lifespan of the sufferer. In a family where one or both parents is sick, the family will lose valuable income and may be forced to sell assets like livestock in order to pay for healthcare and burials. Some societies do not allow widows to inherit land, so it may be lost to the family. Young children may be forced to leave school in order to work or care for sick relatives. The specialised knowledge that parents might have hoped to pass on to their children may be lost.

Where a country is already weakened by epidemics or war, natural phenomena like droughts or floods become far more difficult to overcome. Corruption, mismanagement and bad

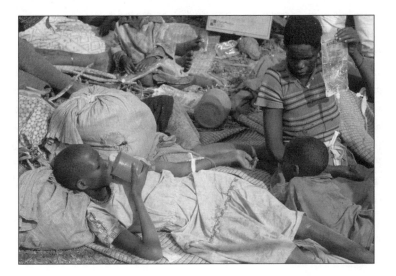

government mean that the country may lack funds to import food when it's needed – so a food shortage can very quickly turn into a famine.

Having enough to eat is a basic human right, and hunger is a huge impediment to development. People who have enough to eat can work better and generate more income. One study in Sierra Leone showed that, on average, a 50 per cent increase in calories per farm worker would increase agricultural output by 16.5 per cent.

So how to achieve this? There are huge surpluses of food in the rich West – so much so, in fact, that food is sometimes destroyed in order to keep prices buoyant. A lot of surplus food is sent to poorer countries as aid, but agencies are well aware that this does not constitute a long-term solution. The key is to change the factors that led to the poverty in the first place: by raising the average income in a region so that hungry people, and in turn their governments, can buy what they need.

In Afghanistan, for example, aid agencies are helping to feed a population ravaged by two decades of war and a severe drought. Some of it has involved distributing food donated by the West, but other initiatives have provided seeds, tools and fertiliser for farmers to grow their own crops. These efforts, coupled with better weather and pest control, meant that the 2003 harvest was forecast to be 50 per cent bigger than the year before. But Christian Aid expressed strong concerns that the UN was still sending massive wheat shipments to the region, causing prices for locally grown wheat to plummet and farmers to turn to more lucrative crops – like opium. The key is not to make countries dependent on handouts, if at all possible; instead, the international community should help guide hunger-stricken societies towards a degree of self-sufficiency. As hunger decreases, the country's income will rise, and it will be better able to cope with food shortages in the future.

But even that path is complicated. African nations are currently debating the role that genetically modified food should play in the fight against hunger. The US has suggested that high-yield GM crops could help the fight against hunger by raising farmers' incomes. There are even suggestions that genetic modification could invent crops that might target micro-nutrient deficiencies. Some countries have enthusiastically welcomed the prospect of GM food aid, while others have declared it 'poison'. There are certainly long-term issues to consider here, not just about the possible effects of GM food on consumers and the environment, but about the culture of dependence that it could create. Poorer countries would become more reliant on developed countries and large multinational companies to supply the GM technology that they cannot afford themselves.

One of the most important factors in reducing hunger is thought to be education. The FAO estimates that some 300 million poor children in the world either do not attend school or do not receive a meal during the school day. Basic education is the most effective development tool there is. In countries with an adult literacy rate of 40 per cent, per capita gross domestic product (GDP) averaged $210; where the rate was at least 80 per cent, per capita GDP was $1,000 and more. Girls who go to school marry later and have fewer children. Farmers who have a minimum of four years' education are up to ten per cent more productive.

The World Food Summit in 1996 set a target of cutting the world's hunger problem in half by 2015. To do that, the number of hungry people needs to fall by 33 million every year – currently, it is only falling by 6 million a year. Progress needs to be accelerated. In October 2003, the World Food Programme noted that contributions to its fund were not keeping pace with the demand for food aid. In 2003, it needed $4.3 billion to feed 110 million people around the world, and contributions fell short by $600 million (or nearly fifteen per cent).

Global bodies like the WHO are urging the world to recognise that proper nutrition and health are fundamental human rights. Combating hunger will allow poorer nations to carve a path towards development. Director-General Emeritus of the WHO, Gro Harlem Brundtland, urged that 'a strong human rights approach is needed to bring on board the millions of people left behind by the 20th century's health revolution'.

Article 25(1) of the Universal Declaration of Human Rights (1948) asserted that 'everyone has the right to a standard of living adequate for the health and well-being of himself and his family, including food'. The human rights approach puts the primary responsibility on governments to do everything possible to ensure people have access to food. But we all have a responsibility to remember the scale of this problem. We can support charities working to promote food security, and we can urge our own governments to do what they can to help – and that includes pressuring them to honour aid commitments.

The victims of famine may occasionally make it onto the front pages or news bulletins, but most victims of hunger go unnoticed. Hunger affects the poor, the powerless. It's a complex problem that requires a huge international effort. We are all responsible, but we can all do something about it.

Further reading

As well as Jessica Williams's powerful book about poverty, debt and crime, you might like to look at Simon Sebag Montefiore's *Speeches that Changed the World* (Quercus, 2006), which contains speeches from the past 2000 years on important issues.

Somebody's Watching You

by Alexandra Campbell

This article by novelist Alexandra Campbell first appeared in the *Daily Telegraph*. It describes her concerns as she realises that even innocent citizens can find themselves easily accused of crimes.

I answered the phone to the policewoman with a cheerful apology. They'd written to me a week earlier regarding an 'incident' at my health club last June. I had moved house in April, and the letter was sent after I'd moved away, so I hadn't got around to answering it. The policewoman, I'll call her DC Smith, informed me that a credit card had been stolen from the ladies' changing room on 16 June. Someone had been seen shopping with it on CCTV[1] nearby. Apparently, my membership photo had been identified by a health club receptionist, who'd accused me of being the woman on the CCTV.

Although I couldn't believe what I was hearing, I began to shake. I'd always thought worrying about civil liberties[2] was for people who had something to hide. If, like me, you've never committed a crime, you don't expect to find yourself in a police station while the police 'disclose all the evidence' to your solicitor, after which, they suggest, you 'discuss how you want to play it'. I was too gob-smacked to point out that I wouldn't be 'playing it', I would be telling the truth.

When I put the phone down, I felt sick. Someone, somewhere believed me capable of theft. While arranging my children's return to school, I frantically checked the family's diaries. We were living in Surrey with my mother, and I'd spent 16 and 17 June in East Sussex with my sister-in-law, Jane, helping her with her newly born twins and toddler, because her nanny was on holiday. My brother and sister-in-law are both

---

[1]**CCTV**   closed-circuit television
[2]**civil liberties**   our rights and freedom as members of society

barristers. My mobile phone records could place me in East Sussex from 8.35am onwards. I couldn't have been anywhere near London at any point. I wrote it all down and, after a sleepless night, faxed the letter to DC Smith and phoned her to check she had it. 'Mm,' she said, cautiously, 'it may help.' She hinted at other evidence against me, to be disclosed to my solicitor before an interview. This would take at least two hours. As I had to travel to London, that was another day's work lost.

We made an appointment. My mouth felt dry and I kept gulping water. Was I being stitched up? What 'other evidence' could there be? 'Don't worry,' said my brother. 'They always imply that.' I engaged a solicitor, a family friend. Already, the meter was ticking. Not only was I losing work time, but I would have to spend hundreds – perhaps thousands – of pounds to prove my innocence. Would I ever get this back? Could I sue? No, said my legal friends. Anyone can accuse anyone if they believe they're acting in the public interest. By this time, I was in shock. I couldn't concentrate and, when my family talked to me, they got a blank stare. I was terribly nervous about the interview.

Suppose the police thought my nerves were a sign of guilt? And what do you wear for an interrogation? Look smart and be judged a rich bitch, stealing credit cards to fund her shopping binges? Look scruffy and a loser? By the time I met Mark, my solicitor, at the police station, I had hardly slept for two days. Logically, nothing could come of it, because I could prove I wasn't even there. But, suddenly, I no longer believed in logic. We met DC Smith, who was clutching faxed signed letters from my brother and sister-in-law, stating that I was with them on 16 and 17 June. She promptly arrested me for 'credit card theft and deception'. Mark asked why she hadn't interviewed me as a voluntary witness and she muttered something about my not having answered her original letter. Mark told me there was no point in making a fuss – we wanted to show the police we were co-operative, not start with an argument.

I was booked in, asked whether I had mental health problems, self-harmed or wanted to see a drugs counsellor. I spent an agonising half hour reading posters about drugs, shootings and murder while DC Smith outlined the 'evidence' to Mark in an interview room. It was not quite as she'd originally explained. What had actually happened was that at 7.40pm there were only two women in the health club changing room. One of them took out her purse, then moved away to answer a mobile phone call. When she came back, the other woman and the purse had gone. She described the suspect as 'about 35 and dark-haired'. I am 50 and have white-blonde hair. The card was used immediately at several shops nearby – a sign of a professional, as they know they have to spend quickly, according to Mark. Two of the shops caught her on CCTV. The victim of the credit card theft somehow persuaded a supermarket to let her view the footage, with a health club receptionist. Neither of them recognised anyone.

However, a week later, I walked into the club and handed the receptionist my swipe card. He suddenly thought I looked like the woman on CCTV and informed the police – in spite of the fact that the club's swipe system on 16 June showed that I wasn't checked in that day. He told the police that their security is so ineffective that anyone can walk in. Why this made it more likely to be me, who has always swiped in, rather than a walk-in thief, I can't imagine. After the receptionist's report, the police interviewed two assistants in one of the other shops, who said they remembered the woman with the stolen credit card, describing her as having brown, untidy hair. They thought she was about 40–45 – older, but, still, the only similarity was the untidiness of my hair.

We were shown two stills from the CCTV. One matched the description given of the suspect by the victim. It looked nothing like me. The other image, which the receptionist saw, was a back view. Her bottom is like mine – a chunky, national-average size 16. Her hair was brown. 'Well,' said DC Smith. 'Blonde, brown, darkish; it's all the same really.' I produced a photograph taken at the end of June 2003 on a date-stamped digital camera to show that my hair was clearly very white-blonde. So far, I seemed to have been arrested for having untidy hair and a big bottom.

I was asked if I would attend an ID parade in front of the shop assistants. I said I would co-operate in any way, but had no faith in the memory of two young men who had served someone in a shop nine months ago. Couldn't they interview my brother and access my mobile phone records first? At this point, I realised they wanted to build a case. As a police friend said later: 'Once you've actually got a suspect sitting in front of you, police instinct is always to work as hard as possible to make the charge stick.'

The police could have dropped the charges at that point, but were suspicious about my ability to give such a full account of how I had spent the two days in question. I explained that my brother's new twins were quite an event, and it would be difficult to forget them. I was bailed to appear two weeks later, fingerprinted and photographed. 'In theory,' said Mark, 'it's innocent until proved guilty. In practice, whoever makes the allegation first is believed.' Now that we are all picked up on CCTVs up to 300 times a day, and can also easily be identified electronically through swipe cards (health clubs, the office,

season tickets, etc.), there is a real risk of someone linking you to a passing resemblance on a fuzzy CCTV image and making an allegation against you.

The police had taken about eight months to get to this point of the inquiry and I was terrified of enduring months' more worry before I was cleared, but they followed up my brother's statement quickly and dropped the charges. However, they told me that current policy is to leave fingerprints, pictures and allegations permanently on file. Checking subsequently with the police press office, I find that 'fingerprints may not be held for more than 42 days', but I find it scary that nobody really seems to know. I suspect our civil rights are being chipped away all the time in the name of crime and terrorism prevention.

The whole thing, I discovered, was based on a breach of the Data Protection Act. Companies using CCTV are supposed to show images only to authorised people, such as the police. The supermarket involved should never have allowed the reception-ist and the credit card victim to see footage on demand. The receptionist, himself in charge of CCTV, should have known this. He wasn't even following his own company's code of prac-tice, which asks staff who are suspicious of members to take the matter to a manager first. But he has done nothing illegal.

And neither have I. But while I struggle to have my records deleted from police files, he has drifted on and cannot, so far, be contacted. Nobody knows if he made the allegation out of boredom, spite, or genuine, if misplaced, civic-mindedness. It's Kafkaesque,[3] said friends. It's a joke, said others. But it wasn't fiction and it wasn't funny. I was actually very lucky. I might not have been able to prove where I was. If I'd been a lawyer, police officer, accountant or worked in financial services, my career and livelihood would also have been on the line, and if I'd been a celebrity, the story would have been splashed all over the papers before it was disproved. If the allegation had been

---

[3]**Kafkaesque**   like the nightmarish worlds described by Franz Kafka

connected to terrorism, I would have been jailed immediately. I used to think that if you didn't break the law, you had nothing to fear from it. Now I know that if this can happen to me, it can happen to anyone.

Further reading

The most powerful novel about constant surveillance in society is George Orwell's *Nineteen Eighty-Four* (Penguin Books Ltd, 2004). You might also enjoy the science fiction stories of Ray Bradbury, which deal with the way society can begin to dominate individuals. Start with *Bradbury Stories: 100 of His Most Celebrated Tales* (Harper Perennial, 2005).

Televised

by Maya Angelou

Maya Angelou (born 1928) is an African-American novelist and poet. She is perhaps best known for her autobiography, *I Know Why the Caged Bird Sings*. In this poem she writes about the way television presents certain issues – such as famine.

Televised news turns
a half-used day into
a waste of desolation.[1]
If nothing wondrous preceded
the catastrophic[2] announcements,
certainly nothing will follow, save
the sad-eyed faces of
bony children,
distended[3] bellies making
mock at their starvation.
Why are they always
Black?
Whom do they await?
The lamb-chop flesh
reeks and cannot be
eaten. Even the
green peas roll on my plate
unmolested. Their innocence
matched by the helpless
hope in the children's faces.
Why do Black children
hope? Who will bring
them peas and lamb chops
and one more morning?

---

[1]**desolation**   complete emptiness or destruction
[2]**catastrophic**   relating to wide-scale disaster and suffering
[3]**distended**   swollen

Further reading

Maya Angelou is best known for her uplifting and fascinating autobiography *I Know Why the Caged Bird Sings* (New Windmill, Heinemann Educational Publishers, 1995). For an interesting alternative perspective on the effects of television (and computer games, movies and other aspects of modern life), try Stephen Johnson's superbly entertaining *Everything Bad for You Is Good for You: How Popular Culture Is Making Us Smarter* (Penguin Books Ltd, 2006).

The Fish Are All Sick

by Anne Stevenson

This poem and the next explore how we treat the planet and our fellow creatures on Earth. Here, Anne Stevenson takes a bleak look at
the way we humans are destroying our environment.

The fish are all sick, the great whales dead,
The villages stranded in stone on the coast,
Ornamental,[1] like pearls on the fringe of a coat.
Sea men, who knew what the ocean did,
Turned their low houses away from the surf.
But new men who come to be rural and safe
Add big glass views and begonia[2] beds.
Water keeps to itself.
White lip after lip
Curls to a close on the littered beach.
Something is sicker and blacker than fish.
And closing its grip, and closing its grip.

Further reading

Anne Stevenson's poems can be read in *Poems 1955–2005* (Bloodaxe
Books Ltd, 2006). You might also like to find out about Greenpeace, an
organisation that campaigns to save the planet (visit www.greenpeace.org/
international/).

---

[1]**ornamental**   for display only
[2]**begonia**   small colourful flower

The Lake

by Roger McGough

Like Anne Stevenson's poem, *The Fish Are All Sick*, *The Lake* is about
pollution. In it, Roger McGough uses fantasy to make his point.

For years there have been no fish in the lake.
People hurrying through the park avoid it
like the plague. Birds steer clear
and the sedge[1] of course has withered.
Trees lean away from it,
and at night it reflects, not the moon,
but the blackness of its own depths.

There are no fish in the lake.
But there is life there. There is life . . .

Underwater pigs glide between reefs of coral debris.
They love it here. They breed and multiply
in sties hollowed out of the mud
and lined with mattresses and bedsprings.
They live on dead fish and rotting things,
drowned pets, plastic and assorted excreta.[2]
Rusty cans they like the best.
Holding them in webbed trotters
their teeth tear easily through the tin,
and poking in a snout, they noisily suck out
the putrid[3] matter within.

There are no fish in the lake.
But there is life there. There is life . . .

[1]**sedge**   a grass-like plant found in wet ground
[2]**excreta**   waste products
[3]**putrid**   rotting

For on certain evenings after dark
shoals of pigs surface
and look out at those houses near the park.
Where, in bathrooms,
children feed stale bread to plastic ducks,
and in attics,
toy yachts have long since runaground.
Where, in livingrooms,
anglers dangle their lines on patterned carpets,
and bemoan[4] the fate of the ones that got away.

Down on the lake, piggy eyes glisten.
They have acquired a taste for flesh.
They are licking their lips. Listen . . .

Further reading

Roger McGough's *Strictly Private: An Anthology of Poetry* (Puffin Books, 1996) remains one of the best anthologies of poems for young people. You can read his own mix of funny and sad poems in *Collected Poems* (Penguin Books Ltd, 2004).

---

[4]**bemoan**   complain about

Before Eden

by Arthur C. Clarke

Sometimes it takes a science fiction story to warn us about the future we are creating. This story was written by the legendary sci-fi writer, Arthur C. Clarke, more than 30 years ago. It takes us far into the future. But the themes it addresses are very modern.

'I guess,' said Jerry Garfield, cutting the engines, 'that this is the end of the line.' With a gentle sigh, the underjets faded out; deprived of its air cushion, the scout ram *Rambling Wreck* settled down upon the twisted rocks of the Hesperian Plateau.

There was no way forward; neither on its jets nor its tractors could S₅ – to give the *Wreck* its official name – scale the escarpment that lay ahead. The South Pole of Venus was only thirty miles away, but it might have been on another planet. They would have to turn back, and retrace their four-hundred-mile journey through this nightmare landscape.

The weather was fantastically clear, with visibility of almost a thousand yards. There was no need of radar to show the cliffs ahead; for once, the naked eye was good enough. The green auroral light,[1] filtering down through clouds that had rolled unbroken for a million years, gave the scene an under-water appearance, and the way in which all distant objects blurred into the haze added to the impression. Sometimes it was easy to believe that they were driving across a shallow sea bed, and more than once Jerry had imagined that he had seen fish floating overhead.

'Shall I call the ship, and say we're turning back?' he asked.

'Not yet,' said Dr Hutchins. 'I want to think.'

Jerry shot an appealing glance at the third member of the crew, but found no moral support there. Coleman was just as bad: although the two men argued furiously half the time, they were both scientists and therefore, in the opinion of a hard-

---

[1]**auroral light**   glowing light, as at dawn

headed engineer-navigator, not wholly responsible citizens. If Cole and Hutch had bright ideas about going forward, there was nothing he could do except register a protest.

Hutchins was pacing back and forth in the tiny cabin, studying charts and instruments. Presently he swung the car's searchlight towards the cliffs, and began to examine them carefully with binoculars. Surely, thought Jerry, he doesn't expect me to drive up there! S_5 was a hover-track, not a mountain goat . . .

Abruptly, Hutchins found something. He released his breath in a sudden explosive gasp, then turned to Coleman.

'Look!' he said, his voice full of excitement. 'Just to the left of that black mark! Tell me what you see.'

He handed over the glasses, and it was Coleman's turn to stare.

'Well I'm damned,' he said at length. 'You were right. There *are* rivers on Venus. That's a dried-up waterfall.'

'So you owe me one dinner at the Bel Gourmet when we get back to Cambridge. With champagne.'

'No need to remind me. Anyway, it's cheap at the price. But this still leaves your other theories strictly on the crackpot level.'

'Just a minute,' interjected Jerry. 'What's all this about rivers and waterfalls? Everyone knows they can't exist on Venus. It never gets cold enough on this steam bath of a planet for the clouds to condense.'

'Have you looked at the thermometer lately?' asked Hutchins with deceptive mildness.

'I've been slightly too busy driving.'

'Then I've news for you. It's down to two hundred and thirty, and still falling. Don't forget – we're almost at the Pole, it's winter-time, and we're sixty thousand feet above the lowlands. All this adds up to a distinct nip in the air. If the temperature drops a few more degrees, we'll have rain. The water will be boiling, of course – but it will be water. And though George won't admit it, this puts Venus in a completely different light.'

'Why?' asked Jerry, though he had already guessed.

'Where there's water, there may be life. We've been in too much of a hurry to assume that Venus is sterile, merely because the average temperature's over five hundred degrees. It's a lot colder here, and that's why I've been so anxious to get to the Pole. There are lakes up here in the highlands, and I want to look at them.'

'But *boiling* water!' protested Coleman. 'Nothing could live in that!'

'There are algae that manage it on Earth. And if we've learned one thing since we started exploring the planets, it's this: wherever life has the slightest chance of surviving, you'll find it. This is the only chance it's ever had on Venus.'

'I wish we could test your theory. But you can see for yourself – we can't go up that cliff.'

'Perhaps not in the car. But it won't be too difficult to climb those rocks, even wearing thermosuits. All we need do is walk a few miles towards the Pole; according to the radar maps, it's fairly level once you're over the rim. We could manage in – oh, twelve hours at the most. Each of us has been out for longer than that, in much worse conditions.'

That was perfectly true. Protective clothing that had been designed to keep men alive in the Venusian lowlands would have an easy job here, where it was only a hundred degrees hotter than Death Valley in midsummer.

'Well,' said Coleman, 'you know the regulations. You can't go by yourself, and someone has to stay here to keep contact with the ship. How do we settle it this time – chess or cards?'

'Chess takes too long,' said Hutchins, 'especially when you two play it.' He reached into the chart table and produced a well-worn pack. 'Cut them, Jerry.'

'Ten of spades. Hope you can beat it, George.'

'So do I. Damn – only five of clubs. Well, give my regards to the Venusians.'

Despite Hutchins' assurance, it was hard work climbing the escarpment. The slope was not too steep, but the weight of oxygen gear, refrigerated thermosuit, and scientific equipment came to more than a hundred pounds per man. The lower gravity – thirteen per cent weaker than Earth's – gave a litle help, but not much, as they toiled up screes, rested on ledges to regain breath, and then clambered on again through the submarine twilight. The emerald glow that washed around them was brighter than that of the full moon on Earth. A moon would have been wasted on Venus, Jerry told himself; it could never have been seen from the surface, there were no oceans for it to rule – and the incessant aurora was a far more constant source of light.

They had climbed more than two thousand feet before the ground levelled out into a gentle slope, scarred here and there by channels that had clearly been cut by running water. After a little searching, they came across a gulley wide and deep enough to merit the name of river bed, and started to walk along it.

'I've just thought of something,' said Jerry after they had travelled a few hundred yards. 'Suppose there's a storm up ahead of us? I don't feel like facing a tidal wave of boiling water.'

'If there's a storm,' replied Hutchins a little impatiently, 'we'll bear it. There'll be plenty of time to reach high ground.'

He was undoubtedly right, but Jerry felt no happier as they continued to climb the gently shelving watercourse. His uneasiness had been growing ever since they had passed over the brow of the cliff and had lost radio contact with the scout car. In this day and age to be out of touch with one's fellow-men was a unique and unsettling experience. It had never happened to Jerry before in all his life; even aboard the *Morning Star*, when they were a hundred million miles from Earth, he could always send a message to his family and get a reply back within minutes. But now a few yards of rock had cut him off from the rest of mankind; if anything happened to them here, no one would ever know, unless some later expedition found their bodies. George would wait for the agreed number of hours; then he would head back to the ship – alone. I guess I'm not really the pioneering type, Jerry told himself. I like running complicated machines, and that's how I got involved in space flight. But I never stopped to think where it would lead, and now it's too late to change my mind . . .

They had travelled perhaps three miles towards the Pole, following the meanders of the river bed, when Hutchins stopped to make observations and collect specimens. 'Still getting colder!' he said. 'The temperature's down to one hundred and ninety-nine. That's far and away the lowest ever recorded on Venus. I wish we could call George and let him know.'

Jerry tried all the wave bands; he even attempted to raise the ship – the unpredictable ups and downs of the planet's ionosphere sometimes made such long-distance reception possible – but there was not a whisper of a carrier wave above the roar and crackle of the Venusian thunderstorms.

'This is even better,' said Hutchins, and now there was real excitement in his voice. 'The oxygen concentration's way up – fifteen parts in a million. It was only five back at the car, and down in the lowlands you can scarcely detect it.'

'But fifteen in a *million*!' protested Jerry. 'Nothing could breathe that!'

'You've got hold of the wrong end of the stick,' Hutchins explained. 'Nothing does breathe it. Something *makes* it. Where do you think Earth's oxygen comes from? It's all produced by life – by growing plants. Before there were plants on Earth, our atmosphere was just like this one – a mess of carbon dioxide and ammonia and methane. Then vegetation evolved and slowly converted the atmosphere into something that animals could breathe.'

'I see,' said Jerry, 'and you think that the same process has just started here?'

'It looks like it. *Something* not far from here is producing oxygen – and plant life is the simplest explanation.'

'And where there are plants,' mused Jerry, 'I suppose you'll have animals, sooner or later.'

'Yes,' said Hutchins, packing his gear and starting up the gulley, 'though it takes a few hundred million years. We may be too soon – but I hope not.'

'That's all very well,' Jerry answered. 'But suppose we meet something that doesn't like us? We've no weapons.'

Hutchins gave a snort of disgust.

'And we don't need them. Have you stopped to think what we look like? Any animal would run a mile at the sight of us.'

There was some truth in that. The reflecting metal foil of their thermosuits covered them from head to foot like flexible, glittering armour. No insects had more elaborate antennae than those mounted on their helmets and back packs, and the wide lenses through which they stared out at the world looked like blank yet monstrous eyes. Yes, there were few animals on Earth that would stop to argue with such apparitions; but any Venusians might have different ideas.

Jerry was still mulling over this when they came upon the lake. Even at that first glimpse, it made him think not of the life they were seeking, but of death. Like a black mirror, it lay amid a fold of the hills; its far edge was hidden in the eternal mist, and ghostly columns of vapour swirled and danced upon its surface. All it needed, Jerry told himself, was Charon's ferry waiting to take them to the other side – or the Swan of Tuonela swimming majestically back and forth as it guarded the entrance to the Underworld . . .

Yet for all this, it was a miracle – the first free water that men had ever found on Venus. Hutchins was already on his knees, almost in an attitude of prayer. But he was only collecting drops of the precious liquid to examine through his pocket microscope.

'Anything there?' Jerry asked anxiously.

Hutchins shook his head.

'If there is, it's too small to see with this instrument. I'll tell you more when we're back at the ship.' He sealed a test tube and placed it in his collecting bag, as tenderly as any prospector who had just found a nugget laced with gold. It might be – it probably was – nothing more than plain water. But it might also be a universe of unknown, living creatures on the first stage of their billion-year journey to intelligence.

Hutchins had walked no more than a dozen yards along the edge of the lake when he stopped again, so suddenly that Garfield nearly collided with him.

'What's the matter?' Jerry asked. 'See something?'

'That dark patch of rock over there. I noticed it before we stopped at the lake.'

'What about it? It looks ordinary enough to me.'

'I think it's grown bigger.'

All his life Jerry was to remember this moment. Somehow he never doubted Hutchins' statement; by this time he could believe anything, even that rocks could grow. The sense of isolation and mystery, the presence of that dark and brooding lake, the never-ceasing rumble of distant storms and the green flickering of the aurora – all these had done something to his mind, had prepared it to face the incredible. Yet he felt no fear; that would come later.

He looked at the rock. It was about five hundred feet away, as far as he could estimate. In this dim, emerald light it was hard to judge distances or dimensions. The rock – or whatever it was – seemed to be a horizontal slab of almost black material, lying near the crest of a low ridge. There was a second, much smaller, patch of similar material near it; Jerry tried to measure and memorise the gap between them, so that he would have some yardstick to detect any change.

Even when he saw that the gap was slowly shrinking, he still felt no alarm – only a puzzled excitement. Not until it had vanished completely, and he realised how his eyes had tricked him, did that awful feeling of helpless terror strike into his heart.

Here there were no growing or moving rocks. What they were watching was a dark tide, a crawling carpet, sweeping slowly but inexorably towards them over the top of the ridge.

The moment of sheer, unreasoning panic lasted, mercifully, no more than a few seconds. Garfield's first terror began to fade as soon as he recognised its cause. For that advancing tide had reminded him, all too vividly, of a story he had read many years ago about the army ants of the Amazon, and the way in which they destroyed everything in their path . . .

But whatever this tide might be, it was moving too slowly to be a real danger, unless it cut off their line of retreat. Hutchins was staring at it intently through their only pair of binoculars; he was the biologist, and he was holding his ground. No point in making a fool of myself, thought Jerry, by running like a scalded cat, if it isn't necessary.

'For heaven's sake,' he said at last, when the moving carpet was only a hundred yards away and Hutchins had not uttered a word or stirred a muscle. 'What *is* it?'

Hutchins slowly unfroze, like a statue coming to life.

'Sorry,' he said. 'I'd forgotten all about you. It's a plant, of course. At least, I suppose we'd better call it that.'

'But its *moving*!'

'Why should that surprise you? So do terrestrial plants. Ever seen speeded-up movies of ivy in action?'

'That still stays in one place – it doesn't crawl all over the landscape.'

'Then what about the plankton plants of the sea? *They* can swim when they have to.'

Jerry gave up; in any case, the approaching wonder had robbed him of words.

He still thought of the thing as a carpet – a deep-pile one, ravelled into tassels at the edges. It varied in thickness as it moved; in some parts it was a mere film; in others, it heaped up to a depth of a foot or more. As it came closer and he could see its texture, Jerry was reminded of black velvet. He wondered what it felt like to the touch, then remembered that it would burn his fingers even if it did nothing else to them. He found himself thinking, in the light-headed nervous reaction that often follows a sudden shock: 'If there *are* any Venusians, we'll never be able to shake hands with them. They'd burn us, and we'd give them frostbite.'

So far the thing had shown no signs that it was aware of their presence. It had merely flowed like the mindless tide that it almost certainly was. Apart from the fact that it climbed over small obstacles, it might have been an advancing flood of water.

And then, when it was only ten feet away, the velvet tide checked itself. On the right and the left, it still flowed forward; but dead ahead it slowed to a halt.

'We're being encircled,' said Jerry anxiously. 'Better fall back, until we're sure it's harmless.'

To his relief, Hutchins stepped back at once. After a brief hesitation, the creature resumed its slow advance and the dent in its front line straightened out.

Then Hutchins stepped forward again – and the thing slowly withdrew. Half a dozen times the biologist advanced, only to retreat again, and each time the living tide ebbed and flowed in synchronism with his movements. I never imagined, Jerry told himself, that I'd live to see a man waltzing with a plant . . .

'Thermophobia,' said Hutchins. 'Purely automatic reaction. It doesn't like our heat.'

'*Our* heat!' protested Jerry. 'Why, we're living icicles by comparison.'

'Of course – but our suits aren't, and that's all it knows about.'

Stupid of me, thought Jerry. When you were snug and cool inside your thermosuit, it was easy to forget that the refrigeration unit on your back was pumping a blast of heat out into the surrounding air. No wonder the Venusian plant had shied away . . .

'Let's see how it reacts to light,' said Hutchins. He switched on his chest lamp, and the green auroral glow was instantly banished by the flood of pure white radiance. Until Man had come to this planet, no white light had ever shone upon the surface of Venus, even by day. As in the seas of Earth, there was only a green twilight, deepening slowly to utter darkness.

The transformation was so stunning that neither man could check a cry of astonishment. Gone in a flash was the deep, sombre black of the thick-pile velvet carpet at their feet. Instead, as far as their lights carried lay a blazing pattern of glorious, vivid reds, laced with streaks of gold. No Persian prince could ever have commanded so opulent[2] a tapestry from his weavers, yet this was the accidental product of biological forces. Indeed, until they had switched on their floods, these superb colours had not even existed, and they would vanish once more when the alien light of Earth ceased to conjure them into being.

'Tikov was right,' murmured Hutchins. 'I wish he could have known.'

'Right about what?' asked Jerry, though it seemed almost sacrilege to speak in the presence of such loveliness.

'Back in Russia, fifty years ago, he found that plants living in very cold climates tended to be blue and violet, while those from hot ones were red or orange. He predicted that the Martian vegetation would be violet, and said that if there were plants on Venus they'd be red. Well, he was right on both counts. But we can't stand here all day – we've work to do.'

'You're quite sure it's safe?' asked Jerry, some of his caution reasserting itself.

'Absolutely – it can't touch our suits even if it wants to. Anyway, it's moving past us.'

That was true. They could see now that the entire creature – if it was a single plant, and not a colony – covered a roughly circular area about a hundred yards across. It was sweeping over the ground, as the shadow of a cloud moves before the wind – and where it had rested, the rocks were pitted with innumerable tiny holes that might have been etched by acid.

'Yes,' said Hutchins, when Jerry remarked about this. 'That's how some lichens feed; they secrete acids that dissolve rock. But no questions, please – not till we get back to the ship. I've several lifetime's work here, and a couple of hours to do it in.'

This was botany on the run . . . The sensitive edge of the huge plant-thing could move with surprising speed when it tried to evade them. It was as if they were dealing with an animated flapjack, an acre in extent. There was no reaction – apart from the automatic avoidance of their exhaust heat – when

---

[2]**opulent**   luxurious

Hutchins snipped samples or took probes. The creature flowed steadily onward over hills and valleys, guided by some strange vegetable instinct. Perhaps it was following some vein of mineral; the geologists could decide that, when they analysed the rock samples that Hutchins had collected both before and after the passage of the living tapestry.

There was scarcely time to think or even to frame the countless questions that their discovery had raised. Presumably these creatures must be fairly common, for them to have found one so quickly. How did they reproduce? By shoots, spores, fission, or some other means? Where did they get their energy? What relatives, rivals, or parasites did they have? This could not be the only form of life on Venus – the very idea was absurd, for if you had one species, you must have thousands . . .

Sheer hunger and fatigue forced them to a halt at last. The creature they were studying could eat its way around Venus – though Hutchins believed that it never went very far from the lake, as from time to time it approached the water and inserted a long, tube-like tendril into it – but the animals from Earth had to rest.

It was a great relief to inflate the pressurized tent, to climb in through the airlock, and strip off their thermosuits. For the first time, as they relaxed inside their tiny plastic hemisphere, the true wonder and importance of the discovery forced itself upon their minds. This world around them was no longer the same; Venus was no longer dead – it had joined Earth and Mars.

For life called to life, across the gulfs of space. Everything that grew or moved upon the face of any planet was a portent, a promise that Man was not alone in this universe of blazing suns and swirling nebulae. If as yet he had found no companions with whom he could speak, that was only to be expected, for the light-years and the ages still stretched before him, waiting to be explored. Meanwhile, he must guard and cherish the life he found, whether it be upon Earth or Mars or Venus.

So Graham Hutchins, the happiest biologist in the solar system, told himself as he helped Garfield collect their refuse and seal it into a plastic disposal bag. When they deflated the tent and started on the homeward journey, there was no sign of the creature they had been examining. That was just as well; they might have been tempted to linger for more experiments, and already it was getting uncomfortably close to their deadline.

No matter; in a few months they would be back with a team of assistants, far more adequately equipped, and with the eyes of the world upon them. Evolution had laboured for a billion years to make this meeting possible; it could wait a little longer.

For a while nothing moved in the greenly glimmering, fog-bound land-scape; it was deserted by man and crimson carpet alike. Then, flowing over the wind-carved hills, the creature reappeared. Or perhaps it was another of the same strange species; no one would ever know.

It flowed past the little cairn of stones where Hutchins and Garfield had buried their wastes. And then it stopped.

It was not puzzled, for it had no mind. But the chemical urges that drove it relentlessly over the polar plateau were crying: Here, here! Somewhere close at hand was the most precious of all the foods it needed – phosphorus, the element without which the spark of life could never ignite. It began to nuzzle the rocks, to ooze into the cracks and crannies, to scratch and scrabble with probing tendrils. Nothing that it did was beyond the capacity of any plant or tree on Earth – but it moved a thou-sand times more quickly, requiring only minutes to reach its goal and pierce through the plastic film.

And then it feasted, on food more concentrated than any it had ever known. It absorbed the carbohydrates and the proteins and the phos-phates, the nicotine from the cigarette ends, the cellulose from the paper cups and spoons. All these it broke down and assimilated into its strange body, without difficulty and without harm.

Likewise it absorbed a whole microcosmos of living creatures – the bacteria and viruses which, upon an older planet, had evolved into a thousand deadly strains. Though only a very few could survive in this heat and this atmosphere, they were sufficient. As the carpet crawled back to the lake, it carried contagion to all its world.

Even as the Morning Star *set course for her distant home, Venus was dying. The films and photographs and specimens that Hutchins was carrying in triumph were more precious even than he knew. They were the only record that would ever exist of life's third attempt to gain a foothold in the solar system.*

Beneath the clouds of Venus, the story of Creation was ended.

Further reading

Arthur C. Clarke's science-fiction stories remain powerful and often chilling. His most famous tale became a mesmerising, ground-breaking film: *2001: A Space Odyssey* (Orbit, 1990). If you want to read more about time travel, try *The Best Time Travel Stories of the 20th Century* (edited by Harry Turtledove and Martin Harry Greenberg; Del Rey Books, 2004).

Activities

The Destructors

Before you read

1   This story is set in the mid 20th century, around 1950. What do you know about life then? Working in a small group, use a spider diagram to jot down as many details as you can. Think about what was going on in Britain and the world at the time as well as what the clothes and everyday items were like.

What's it about?

2   Read the story, then make some notes on what you learn about the main characters. Include details of their appearance, their background and their behaviour/attitude/habits. You might use a table to organise your notes.

3   How sympathetic (sorry for or on his side) does the writer make us feel for Mr Thomas? Give your answer as a score out of 10, with 10 meaning 'very sympathetic'. Explain your score in one sentence.

Thinking about the text

4   Use these questions to explore the character of T:
   a   T says about Mr Thomas: 'Of course I don't hate him . . . There'd be no fun if I hated him.' Explain what you think he means.
   b   When the others want to give up, T says that they must carry on. What do you think motivates him?
   c   Some readers think T is evil. Do you agree? How do you explain his behaviour?

5   Look at the language Graham Greene uses in the story. What do you notice about:
   a   how the different characters speak?
   b   how the writer describes people and places?
   c   how he builds a sense of tension?

6   Imagine that, after the story ends, Mr Thomas and the boys who destroyed his house are brought face to face with each other. What would the boys say to justify what they have done? How would Mr Thomas treat them? Working in a small group, devise and perform a role play in which they are all present, perhaps at a meeting organised by the police or a social worker.

We Are Going to See the Rabbit

Before you read

1 What is your opinion of zoos? Are they a good way of letting people see endangered species, or – in an age where we can see those creatures in high-definition quality on television – are they no longer necessary? Make a two-column list showing the arguments for and against zoos. Discuss your ideas with the rest of your class.

What's it about?

Read the poem and answer questions 2 to 4 by yourself. Then compare your answers with a partner's.

2 Where is the rabbit kept, and why?

3 Why do you think the police are there?

4 Why does the rabbit disappear?

Thinking about the text

5 The poet uses quite a lot of repetition and there are several lists. Use these questions to explore why he does this. Write a sentence or two in answer to each question.

    a The most obvious repetition is the frequent use of the word 'rabbit'. Why do you think it is used so often? What is the effect of this repetition?

    b The second section of the poem describes the journey to see the rabbit. It is quite repetitive and lists all the stages of the journey. What effect does this have? Why do you think the poet chooses to do this?

6 Imagine you were one of the young children taken to see the rabbit that day, only to find that it had gone. What are your memories of the day? Write a short diary entry describing what it was like. You could start like this:

I had been looking forward to seeing the rabbit a lot. For weeks people had been talking about it, telling me that there would be crowds of people . . .

Song of the Battery Hen

Before you read

1   What do you know about factory farming? Why are chickens kept in small cages rather than being allowed to wander free? Write a short paragraph to explain what you understand by the term.

What's it about?

Read the poem and answer questions 2 and 3 by yourself. Then discuss your answers in a small group.

2   How would you describe the character of the hen who narrates the poem? Choose two or three words that you think describe her from the list below.

angry	upset	dim	naïve	cross
aggressive	accepting	grateful	optimistic	

Write a sentence explaining each of your choices.

3   What picture do you get of the conditions the hens are being kept in? Write a summary.

Thinking about the text

4   The hen who narrates the poem feels that she is an individual. Use these questions to explore how true this is.

   a   Write down a line or phrase from the poem that shows that the hen feels that she is an individual. Explain your choice.

   b   Based on the description in the poem, draw a sketch of what the hen looks like and where she is.

   c   Write down a line or phrase from the poem that shows that the hen's world is actually very impersonal and not at all individual. Explain your choice.

   d   Write a short paragraph explaining why the hen sees herself differently from how we see her and how the poet conveys this.

5   Imagine a gloomy, more cynical hen who does not value the conditions she's kept in. Write an alternative version of the poem in which this second hen complains about the cruelty and horror of the hen house.

Alexander Graham Bell and the Telephone

Before you read

1   Which scientific or technological invention (e.g. car, computer, phone, television) do you rely on the most? Which invention could you most easily do without? Write a short paragraph explaining each of your choices. Compare your answers with a partner's.

What's it about?

2   Read the extract and answer these questions.

    a   Even as a young man, Alexander Graham Bell showed himself to be inventive. Write down two things he developed before he invented the telephone.

    b   What do we learn from the text about Alexander Graham Bell's background? Write down some facts about his family and where they lived.

    c   What was *Visible Speech* designed to do?

3   Use a diagram to show how Bell's idea for the telephone worked. Label it to show the main elements of the invention.

4   Choose the word you think best describes Alexander Graham Bell:

    eccentric   *creative*   *determined*   *curious*   *kind*

    Write a sentence explaining your choice.

Thinking about the text

5   This is a very factual piece of writing. Look more closely at the language and find examples of words that fit these categories:

- simple words
- complex words
- familiar, everyday words
- technical words.

Based on your analysis of the language, at whom do you think the text is aimed – people who already know about science or general readers? Write a sentence to explain your view.

6   Take the information in Adam Hart Davis and Paul Bader's article and transform it into a fact-sheet for 10-year-olds which tells them about:

- Alexander Graham Bell
- how the telephone works
- the impact his invention had.

Make your fact-sheet clear, eye-catching and easy to follow.

Hunger

Before you read

1   This poem takes the form of a riddle such as we sometimes hear in childhood. Riddles were popular in Anglo-Saxon times. This riddle is from that period:

> *A wonder on the wave, water became bone. What am I?*

(The answer is at the bottom of page 225.)

Working in a small group, make up your own riddle. See whether another group can work out what you are describing.

What's it about?

2   The poet uses a variety of images to compare hunger to other things – for example 'I come among the peoples like a shadow'. Choose two of the images and draw a sketch of the picture they create in your mind.

3   Write down what you understand by each of these lines:
   a   *I sit down by each man's side.*
   b   *I am more feared than cannon.*
   c   *I unswear words, and undo deeds.*
   d   *I am first and last to be felt of the living.*

Thinking about the text

4   Think of a reply to Hunger's words. Write an imaginary letter to Hunger telling him of the damage he is doing to the world, why he should not feel proud and why the world would be better without him. Tell him why you hope the world will one day destroy him. Make your letter direct, powerful and emotional. Sneer and poke fun at Hunger. Use a combination of short and long sentences.

5   Choose another threat to people in the world. It might be global warming, drug trafficking, AIDS, terrorism, or something else. Use the format of Laurence Binyon's poem to write a poem of your own – use the first person ('I') and hold back the name of your topic to the very end.

Fast Food Nation

Before you read

1   Politicians, doctors and others say we must do something to stop Britain's unhealthy eating habits. Changes have already been made to the rules about what sorts of foods can be advertised on television when children might be watching and about what sorts of food can be sold in schools. Other people think that what children eat is not their school's responsibility. Hold a class debate about the arguments for and against further legislation aimed at controlling what children eat.

What's it about?

2   Read the extract and answer these questions.
   a Why, according to the author, did customers used to like McDonald's French fries so much?
   b Why did McDonald's switch to using vegetable oil for frying in 1990.
   c Why do you think the flavour industry is so secretive?
   d Write down five facts about food flavouring that you have learned from the article.

3   Eric Schlosser describes the way our bodies taste and smell different flavours. Draw a diagram of a human head and label it to explain the process of taste and smell.

Thinking about the text

4   Can you tell what Eric Schlosser thinks of artificial flavours? Is he opposed to them, or does he take a neutral view and not show us what he thinks? Find a sentence that shows him just giving facts. Find another that shows his own viewpoint. What differences are there in the language used in the two sentences?

5   Imagine you are a senior director of McDonald's and you object to what Eric Schlosser has said about your products. Write a letter to him saying why you think his book is unfair.

Facts to Change the World

Before you read

1   We often see images of people starving in developing countries in the news. Events such at the Live Aid and Live8 concerts (held in 1985 and 2005) aim to raise money and shape people's opinions. What else do you think people in the wealthy West could do to help people in the developing countries? Pool your ideas and make a class poster explaining what could be done.

What's it about?

2   Read the extract and answer these questions.
   a   Write down five facts have you learned from reading the extract.
   b   What does expert Amartya Sen say is the cause of the problem?
   c   Write down a statistic that shows that if a country's people eat well the whole country achieves more.

3   The text finishes positively – reminding us that we can do something about world hunger. Write down between three and five things that the extract suggests we could do to help.

Thinking about the text

4   Put each of these sentences into your own words. Then write a sentence or two explaining the meaning and effect of the words in bold.
   a   *Hunger is also, **callously**, used as a tool of war.*
   b   *Where a country is already **weakened** by epidemics or war, natural phenomena like droughts or floods become far more difficult to overcome.*
   c   *We are all **responsible**, but we can all do something about it.*

5   Get into a small group. Imagine that you are going to go before the United Nations to explain why we should be doing more to help those countries that are battling with hunger. How would you persuade the UN panel to take you seriously? Which statistics and arguments would you use? Imagine that another group is the UN and present your case.

Somebody's Watching You

Before you read

1   What do you think about the use of closed-circuit television (CCTV) in towns and cities? Discuss the arguments for and against the use of CCTV with the rest of your class.

What's it about?

Read the extract and answer questions 2 and 3 by yourself. Then discuss your ideas in a small group.

2   Alexandra Campbell's story starts off simply enough. Make a list of the events that make her realise that she is in trouble. Your list should start like this:

> Stage 1 — Telephone call from police, informing her that she has been identified as a thief.

3   What is the evidence that proves that Alexandra Campbell could not have been the thief? Imagine you are Alexandra and write a short statement explaining why you are innocent.

Thinking about the text

4   Look more closely at the language the writer uses.

   a   First examine some of the very informal language she uses and think of other, more formal, expressions that she might have used.
   - *I was too **gob-smacked** to point out that I wouldn't be 'playing it'*
   - *Was I being **stitched up**?*
   - *Look smart and be judged a **rich bitch***

   b   Now find a sentence in which the writer uses much more formal language.

   c   Write a short paragraph explaining why you think she uses this mix of styles – what effect does it have?

5   Alexandra Campbell says: 'if I'd been a celebrity, the story would have been splashed all over the papers before it was disproved'. Imagine that she is a celebrity and you are a journalist. Write the first 150 words of the story. Set it out as if it is on the front page of your newspaper: write a headline and decide what image you would try to obtain to illustrate your story.

Televised

Before you read

1   Some people say young people should not be allowed to have televisions in their bedrooms. What do you think? Write a short paragraph explaining your opinion.

What's it about?

2   Read the poem through and then look again at the first sentence of the poem. What is the poet saying about the effect of television?

3   Use these questions to explore the imagery of the poem.

   a   In her description of suffering children, Maya Angelou uses the following phrase:

   distended bellies making mock / at their starvation.

   Re-write the phrase in your own words, then write a sentence or two explaining what you think the poet means by 'making mock'.

   b   Suddenly the focus of the poem switches to the food that the narrator is attempting to eat – lamb chop and green peas. What point does she make by comparing her life with the suffering children's?

Thinking about the text

4   What do you think are the main messages of the poem? Read the statements below and decide how strongly you agree with them – give each a score out of 10, with 10 meaning 'completely agree'. The poem is saying that:

   a   television is bad
   b   television is powerful
   c   television can change our views
   d   starvation is terrible
   e   we don't know how lucky we are
   f   we often feel helpless when confronted with people's suffering.

   Which statement did you give the highest score? Write a sentence or two explaining why.

5   The message of Maya Angelou's poem could be written as an article. Would it have more or less impact? Write the opening paragraph of an article in which you try to persuade your audience about the effects of television. Then write a sentence or two comparing your new text with Maya Angelou's poem.

The Fish Are All Sick

Before you read

1   Many of us worry about what the future will be like. Global warming, a shortage of oil, war and terrorism are all common worries. What is your biggest fear about the future? Write a short paragraph explaining your answer.

What's it about?

2   Anne Stevenson's poem shows how a landscape has been changed. Read the poem, then use a two-column table to record what it was like before and what it is like now.

3   What do you think is the poem's message? Sum it up in one sentence.

4   The ending of the poem is threatening and menacing. Write down what you think is going to happen.

Thinking about the text

5   Does the poem give you the impression that the people are deliberately destroying the landscape, or is what is happening simply the effect of the way they are living? Discuss your ideas in a small group.

6   Look more closely at the language of the poem.
   a   Write a sentence explaining in your own words what each of these phrases mean:
   - *villages . . . like pearls on the fringe of a coat*
   - *Water keeps to itself*
   - *Something is sicker and blacker than fish.*
   b   What is the effect of each image? What does it make you think of? Write a short paragraph explaining why you think Anne Stevenson chose these images.

7   Imagine you are someone who owns one of the houses, and you are about to move. What would you say in your advertisement to attract people to come and look around your home? What are the attractions and benefits? What would you *not* mention? Write a 100-word advertisement.

The Lake

Before you read

1   Many people hate litter and pollution. Think of three practical suggestions for reducing litter at your school. Pool your ideas and use the best to make a class poster encouraging people not to drop litter.

What's it about?

Read the poem and answer questions 2 to 4 by yourself. Then compare your answers with a partner's.

2   Roger McGough imagines underwater pigs feeding on the debris left by humans. Draw a picture of what the pigs look like and how they behave. Label it with details from the poem.

3   The human beings in the poem lead tame and tedious lives. Write down two phrases that show humans living a life that has lost its adventure.

4   Look at the ending of the poem. What do you think the writer is suggesting is going to happen next?

Thinking about the text

5   Is this a poem or a list of points? Make a list of the features you would expect to find in a poem and decide in what ways *The Lake* feels like a poem, and in what ways it doesn't. Think about these elements:

* repetition of words, letters and sounds
* rhythm
* rhyme
* the way in which ideas are structured.

6   Imagine you have just been sitting at the side of the lake and have noticed the underwater pigs for the first time. Write an e-mail to a friend describing what you saw and what you think you should do about the problem.

Before Eden

Before you read

1   Some people believe that the human race should spend lots of money on space travel; others believe we would be better off solving the problems we have here on Earth. What are the arguments for and against exploring space further? Discuss your ideas with the rest of your class.

What's it about?

2   Read the story and write a sentence or two in answer to each of these questions:
   a   Why is the spacecraft known as the *Rambling Wreck*?
   b   Why does the crew think they will have to turn back, even though they are so close to their destination?
   c   What do we learn from the story about what Venus is like?
   d   In particular, what is the plant Jerry and Hutchins find like?
   e   What does his first glimpse of the lake make Jerry think of?
   f   Hutchins believes that 'he must guard and cherish the life he found, whether it be upon Earth or Mars or Venus'. So what goes wrong?

3   Get into a group of three and allocate each person one of the three characters (Jerry, Dr Hutchins and Coleman). Imagine that you are on the spacecraft and Jerry has just said: 'Shall I call the ship, and say we're turning back?' Devise a role play that shows what each character is thinking and feeling at this point in the story. Try to get right inside your character's head. Ask yourself these questions:
   ●   What does your character think about the other two characters?
   ●   What does your character think is going to happen next?

Thinking about the text

4   To create the feeling of a future world, the writer uses a number of technical terms that we wouldn't use today. Write down three examples. How else does the writer use language to make the reader believe that this story is taking place in the future? Write a short paragraph explaining how successful you think he is, and why.

5   What do you think is the message or moral of this story? Why do you think Arthur C. Clarke chose to call it *Before Eden*? Discuss your ideas in a small group.

Compare and contrast

1   The world we see in some of the texts in this section is rather bleak and depressing. Copy the scale below and decide where on the line you would place each text.

← ─── →

Positive/optimistic   Negative/pessimistic

Compare your completed scale with a partner's.

2   Compare Anne Stevenson's poem *The Fish Are All Sick* with Roger McGough's *The Lake*. List the ways in which the two poems are similar, and the ways in which they are different. Think about:
   ● what the poems are about
   ● their language
   ● their structure.

3   Choose two of the non-fiction texts and compare how they are written using the table below; answer each question by putting a tick in either column 2 or column 3.

		Text A	Text B
a	Which text contains more facts?		
b	Which text contains simpler words?		
c	Which text uses more description?		
d	Which text has the more impersonal tone?		
e	Which text do you like more?		

Write a short paragraph explaining your choice in part e.

4   Choose three or four of the texts. Think about how they might be presented in a different form. For example, a poem about the environment could be a newspaper article or poster; a newspaper article could be a chat-show interview. Think about how the message of the text would be different in the new form. Copy and complete the table below.

Text	Current form (e.g. poem, article, story)	New form (e.g. poem, chat show, film)	How the message would be changed

(Riddle answer for question 1 on page 217: *ice on water.*)

Notes on authors

Maya Angelou (1928–) is an American poet and actress and an important figure in the civil rights movement. She is best known for her autobiographical writings, *I Know Why the Caged Bird Sings* (1969) and *All God's Children Need Traveling Shoes* (1986), and for her poetry collection, *Just Give Me a Cool Drink of Water 'fore I Diiie* (1971).

Tony Anthony (1969–) is a three-times World Kung Fu champion and has worked as a bodyguard for some of the world's most powerful people. *Taming the Tiger* (2004) is the story of how his belief in Jesus Christ changed his life following a period in prison.

Andrea Ashworth (1969–) was born in Manchester. She now works as a research fellow at Jesus College, Oxford. Her upbringing is described in her memoir, *Once in a House on Fire* (1998).

Laurence Binyon (1869–1943) was an English poet, playwright and art scholar, best known for his World War I poetry – *For the Fallen* is often used in Remembrance Sunday services. He was too old to enlist to fight, but went to the Western Front in 1916 to work as a medical orderly with a Red Cross Ambulance Unit.

Richard Branson (1950–) is a British businessman and entrepreneur best known for his Virgin empire, which embraces music, aircraft, mobile phones and trains. A dyslexic, he left school at 16 but went on to become one of the richest men in the world. He is said to have run one of his first businesses from a telephone box.

Edwin Brock (1927–1997) was an English poet. Shortly after World War II, he spent two years in the Royal Navy. He is best known for *Five Ways to Kill a Man*, a poem which highlights the harshness of war and the dehumanising effect of killing. He also wrote a novel and an autobiography.

Alan Brownjohn (1931–) is an English poet and novelist. He worked as a teacher and lecturer before deciding to write full-time. He was Chairman of the Poetry Society between 1982 and 1988 and is a Distinguished Supporter of the British Humanist Association.

Alexandra Campbell is an experienced journalist and novelist. She has written five novels, including *Remember This* (2005), a family saga, and several radio plays. She has also written for a range of newspapers and magazines.

Arthur C. Clarke (1917–) is a novelist best known for his science fiction stories, in particular *2001: A Space Odyssey* (1968) which later became a powerful film directed by Stanley Kubrick. As a boy, Clarke enjoyed stargazing and was an avid reader of science-fiction magazines.

Danny Danziger is an award-winning columnist for *The Sunday Times* and is the author of several books on history and art. His book of interviews with old Etonians, *Eton Voices* (1988), was a best-seller.

Ken Dornstein (1963–) is an American journalist and writer. He lives near Boston with his wife and two children.

U. A. Fanthorpe (1929–) taught English at Cheltenham Ladies' College for 16 years, before leaving to train as a counsellor and to work as a secretary, receptionist and hospital clerk. Her first volume of poetry, *Side Effects*, was published in 1978. In 1994 she became the first woman in 315 years to be nominated for the post of Professor of Poetry at Oxford.

Malcolm Gladwell (1963–) was born in England and raised in Canada. He now lives in New York City, where he is a staff writer for the *New Yorker*. In 2005 he was named as one of the 100 Most Influential People by *Time* magazine.

Robert Graves (1895–1985) was an English poet, novelist and playwright. He produced more than 140 works during his lifetime, the most famous being *Goodbye to All That* (1929), his memoir of World War I, and the novel, *I Claudius* (1934).

Graham Greene (1904–1991) was an English novelist, playwright and short-story writer. He first worked as a journalist and even after he had become a successful novelist he continued to supplement his income by writing film and book reviews. Some of his novels, including *Brighton Rock* (1938), are often referred to as modern classics.

Adam Hart-Davis (1943–) is an English author, historian and television presenter best known for his television programmes on history and science. He studied Chemistry at university, then worked for Oxford University Press, editing science texts and chess manuals. Since 1977 he has worked in television, as a researcher, producer and presenter.

Rudyard Kipling (1865–1936) was a British author and poet. Born in India, he spent much of his childhood living in Portsmouth with a couple who took in the children of British nationals living in India. He is perhaps best known today for his *The Jungle Book* (1894) and his poems about World War I, in which he lost his only son.

Robert Lacey is a British historian best known for his biographies of members of the royal family. He takes research seriously, sometimes even living alongside his subjects: when writing *The Kingdom* (1981), a study of Saudi Arabia, he and his family lived in the desert beside the Red Sea in Jeddah for eighteen months.

Philip Larkin (1922–1985) was an English poet, novelist and occasional journalist (he wrote about jazz for *The Observer*). Considered one of the greatest English poets of the late 20th century, he combined his writing with lifelong service as a librarian. His poetry often celebrates everyday features of English life.

Doris Lessing (1919–) was born in Persia and grew up in Southern Rhodesia (now Zimbabwe). She had a difficult childhood and her formal education ended at 13, when she dropped out of school. She published her first novel, *The Grass Is Singing*, in 1950 and has since written over 50 titles, including poetry, short stories and science fiction.

Penelope Lively (1933–) is an author of short stories and novels for children and adults. Her best-known children's story is probably, *The Ghost of Thomas Kempe* (1973), for which she received the Carnegie Medal. She has also won the Whitbread Award (1976) and the Booker Prize (1987). She is a Fellow of the Royal Society of Literature, and was awarded the OBE in 1989 and the CBE in 2001.

Henry Wadsworth Longfellow (1807–1882) was an American poet and academic well known for his translations of foreign literature as well as his own work. He was one of the 'Fireside Poets', so named because they were the first American poems to be widely popular – and read by the fire. One of his most famous poems is the epic, *The Song of Hiawatha* (1855).

Lyn MacDonald is an English military historian best known for her books about World War I. They are all based on eyewitness accounts. She has also written and acted as historical adviser for several documentaries for television and radio. She is married and lives in London.

Roger McGough (1937–) is an English performance poet and radio presenter from Liverpool. He became famous in the 1960s and 1970s as one of the 'Liverpool Poets' and worked on the dialogue for the Beatles' film, *Yellow Submarine*. In 1999 he won the Cholmondeley Award for poetry and in 2004 he was awarded the CBE.

Leslie Norris (1921–2006) was one of the most important Welsh writers of the last 60 years. Until 1974 he worked as a college lecturer, teacher and headmaster; after 1974 he wrote full-time, although in 1983 he taught for six months at Brigham Young University in Utah, USA, and was later appointed the official Poet-in-Residence at the university.

Ben Okri (1959–) is a Nigerian poet and novelist whose work is well known for its vivid description. He spent his early childhood in London and later returned to England to study at the University of Essex. His novel, *The Famished Road* (1991), won the Booker Prize in 1991, and in 2001 he was an awarded the OBE.

George Orwell (1903–1950) was a British author and journalist. During his lifetime he was best known for his essays, reviews and books of reportage such as *The Road to Wigan Pier* (1937), which describes the living conditions of the poor in the north of England. Now, however, he is best known for his novels, *Animal Farm* (1945) and *Nineteen Eighty-Four* (1949), from which the phrases 'Big Brother', 'Room 101' and 'thought police' have all come.

M13 10249 £ 5.95

Vic Reeves (1959–) is an English comedian best known for *Shooting Stars* (BBC TV). Before making it as a comedian he worked as a pig farmer, cabbage farmer, factory inspector and civil servant. In 2005 Vic Reeves and Bob Mortimer were voted the ninth greatest comedy act ever by fellow comedians.

Eric Schlosser (1959–) is an American journalist best known for his investigative work. He started his career in journalism at *The Atlantic Monthly*, and has also written for *Rolling Stone*, *Vanity Fair*, *The Nation* and *The New Yorker*. His book, *Fast Food Nation* (2002), started life as a two-part article in *Rolling Stone* magazine.

Anne Stevenson (1933–) was born in England and grew up in America. She has written over a dozen volumes of poetry and was the first winner of the Northern Rock Writers Award for writers in the north of England. She has also written several books of essays and literary criticism and a controversial biography of the American poet Sylvia Plath, *Bitter Fame: A Life of Sylvia Plath* (1989).

Rabindranath Tagore (1861–1941) was a Bengali poet, novelist and composer. He started writing poems at the age of eight and went on to become Asia's first Nobel laureate when he won the Nobel Prize in literature in 1913. He is credited with reshaping Bengali literature and music in the late 19th and early 20th centuries.

Oscar Wilde (1854–1900) was an Irish playwright, poet and novelist, best known for his play, *The Importance of Being Earnest* (1895). He attracted controversy all his life, but said 'There is only one thing in the world that is worse than being talked about, and that is not being talked about.'

Jessica Williams is a journalist and producer with the BBC who has produced documentaries on a range of subjects.